"Bridgette's personal story of tragedy, pain, emotional challenges and then triumph is a riveting story to read. I was impressed with the author's ability to reach the heart and soul of the reader. Her ability to speak openly and honestly about her needs and her desires and giving the reader a heart-felt reason why she stumbled drew me into her real-life story right away. I recommend this book to anyone who has struggled, made some mistakes but has had a hard time forgiving oneself. Everyone has been knocked to the ground, so this story should be a wonderful and inspirational read.

"I hope Bridgette continues to speak out about her pains, the mistakes, the understanding that there is more to life than just our personal desires. The author is a strong woman, someone we all need to listen to and learn from and hopefully some day, after we forgive ourselves from the mistakes we have made, to have a more fulfilling life. I love the author's honesty and vulnerability. Haven't we all felt vulnerable and alone? Bridgette has written one of the most heart-felt, true stories—and found a path of happiness after forgiveness."

— Michael John Sullivan, author of *Everybody's Daughter*

"With the book *Fallen Angel Rising*, the author Bridgette allows readers a close and personal look into her life. She not only shares her triumphs but her tragedies, as well. …I have to commend the author for exposing her innermost feelings, and telling them in such a conversational way that not only allowed me to connect with the story, but also to feel as if the author was a dear friend by the end of the book. …A true victim-to-victory story that leaves me wishing the author the best, and also wondering where life's journey will take this remarkable person next."

— Brenda C. for Readers Favorite

Fallen Angel
RISING

BRIDGETTE C. KENT

BALBOA.
PRESS
A DIVISION OF HAY HOUSE

Balboa Press books may be ordered through booksellers or by contacting:

Balboa Press
A Division of Hay House
1663 Liberty Drive
Bloomington, IN 47403
www.balboapress.com
1 (877) 407-4847

Because of the dynamic nature of the Internet, any web addresses or links contained in this book may have changed since publication and may no longer be valid. The views expressed in this work are solely those of the author and do not necessarily reflect the views of the publisher, and the publisher hereby disclaims any responsibility for them.

The author of this book does not dispense medical advice or prescribe the use of any technique as a form of treatment for physical, emotional, or medical problems without the advice of a physician, either directly or indirectly. The intent of the author is only to offer information of a general nature to help you in your quest for emotional and spiritual well-being. In the event you use any of the information in this book for yourself, which is your constitutional right, the author and the publisher assume no responsibility for your actions.

Any people depicted in stock imagery provided by Thinkstock are models, and such images are being used for illustrative purposes only.
Certain stock imagery © Thinkstock.

Print information available on the last page.

ISBN: 978-1-4525-7734-0 (sc)
ISBN: 978-1-4525-7735-7 (e)

Balboa Press rev. date: 7/10/2013

TABLE OF CONTENTS

Foreword   ix

With Gratitude   xi

Preface   xiii

Prologue   xvii

PART 1 | DISCOVERY & CONNECTION

Chapter 1:   The Water Bug   3

Chapter 2:   Finally, Real friends!   7

Chapter 3:   Switching to Shows   14

Chapter 4:   You Can't Make This Stuff Up!   18

Chapter 5:   Not Exactly Feeling Cheerful   21

Chapter 6:   Welcome to High School   23

Chapter 7:   Cracks in My Armor   28

Chapter 8:   Starting Again   32

PART 2 | LOVE HURTS

Chapter 9:   I'll Never Be Me Again   37

Chapter 10:   Life After   40

Chapter 11:   Spreading My Wings   44

Chapter 12:   Life Goes On   49

Chapter 13:   No Really. You Can't Make This Stuff Up!   52

Chapter 14:   Lightning in a Bottle   57

PART 3 | A RUDE AWAKENING

Chapter 15:   Time to Grow Up—or is It?   65

Chapter 16:   Alone / Together   72

Chapter 17:   I'm Not Sure if I Do   75

Chapter 18: Repairing the Damage   78
Chapter 19: Would've, Should've, Could've   81
Chapter 20: Far from Home and All Alone   84
Chapter 21: The Line in the Sand   89

PART 4 | STEPPING OUT

Chapter 22: Born Again!   95
Chapter 23: Bull What?   98
Chapter 24: My New Life   101
Chapter 25: Just Like Riding a Bike   106
Chapter 26: Dream Job Turned Nightmare   110
Chapter 27: Saved by the Bell   117
Chapter 28: Making Money Doing What I Love   124
Chapter 29: Swept Off My Feet at Sea   127
Chapter 30: Man of My Dreams Up in Smoke   131
Chapter 31: This is 911, and We Have an Emergency   137

PART 5 | A SPIRAL DOWN

Chapter 32: Falling like a Brick   143
Chapter 33: Life in "The Bin"   146
Chapter 34: You Can't Hide Forever   151
Chapter 35: Breathe In, Breathe Out   155
Chapter 36: Down Down Down   159
Chapter 37: Going Going Gone   162
Chapter 38: My Dream Destroyed   166
Chapter 39: Doctor Danger   168

PART 6 | TRANSFORMATION

Chapter 40: Facing Facts   175
Chapter 41: New Beginnings   178

Chapter 42: With Each Ending Comes a New Beginning   183
Chapter 43: A Lesson in Forgiveness   188

PART 7 | I AM WHO I AM

Chapter 44: Living It Up!   195
Chapter 45: Back to Reality   200
Chapter 46: Positive Reinforcements   202
Chapter 47: The World Doesn't Come on a Silver Platter, but It
            Does Come with a Silver Lining   205
Chapter 48: Am I Healthy, Wealthy, and Successful?   209
Chapter 49: What I've Learned, What I Believe, and What's Next? 211

Appendix: Final thoughts on Depression & Suicide   213
About the Author   217

FOREWORD

by Hemal Radia
Author of *Find You & You Find Everything:*
The Secrets to the Law of Attraction

It is a true honor for me to be writing this foreword to Bridgette's story—her story so far. I am also honored to be mentioned in this courageous true story. I expect you'll be hearing much more about Bridgette in the future.

The writing of this book has taken bravery and courage. Delving into a past that was not always comfortable, and sharing aspects of it—at times in detail so that others can benefit from mistakes made and insights learned as a consequence, is honorable. There was also courage in the awareness—and understandable concern—that those closest to her would be privy to information and experiences they would not have known and which may not be comfortable for them to know.

Bridgette has experienced extreme situations in her life, taken responsibility—which, in itself, means taking back one's own power—and moved in the direction that she intends for her life. Through all that she has experienced, she has become more aware of herself and the patterns that were in her life. In doing so and by sharing them here, she offers you the opportunity to move towards your own empowerment.

In the time I have known Bridgette, it has been a true passion for her to write from a place of authenticity in sharing this message. Perhaps it is a similar desire to the one that is within you, which has you seeking what you are about to read. Bridgette has taken her own experiences and has chosen to share them with the world to help those who may have experienced—or are experiencing—what she has: to light a path ahead for them. Each of us has our own path to make. Bridgette shares hers, and in doing so, provides the awareness for others that there *is* a path ahead. That, in itself, is empowering.

Bridgette considered writing this as fiction to avoid sharing the "true" details, but she felt it would not have had the impact and authenticity that this book has. Because of how she has chosen to share this with you, you get to experience and know things as they were.

Bridgette wants you to know that all is not lost—whatever your situation is. It does not matter if they are the exact same situations that Bridgette experienced or that you have your own cross to bear; she would tell you that the answers *are* possible. They appear when you open yourself up to them. When I met Bridgette she was seeking hope for her situation. When you are open to your hope or answers, they find a way to you. They can't find the way if you are not open to them. It doesn't matter how long you have endured your situation; it only takes a split moment for things to change. And when they do, they provide a crack of possibility...which gets bigger and bigger...until you get to a point where your life is becoming filled with them.

Thank you to Bridgette for sharing her true story, and wishing you the best on your journey. May it be even more amazing than you think is possible.

Hemal Radia
"Super" Mentor, Speaker,
Author of *Find You & You Find Everything:*
The Secrets to the Law of Attraction
www.hemalradia.com

WITH GRATITUDE

So many people made this book possible, and I cannot possibly thank them all! However, I would like to mention a number of important individuals. Without these people, this book would not have become a reality.

First and foremost: Thank you my *amazing family* for loving me "anyway!" You always had faith and saw the best in me. You always let me know that I was capable of greatness. I draw all of my strength and security from you and love you more than you could ever know!

- *Linda:* You have been my rock for so long—no words can express what your friendship has meant to me! You helped mold me into the person I am. I will always love you like my true sister, and I am forever grateful.
- *Jonah:* Thanks for always being there as one of my most trusted and loyal friends. I can always count on you to "tell it like it is!"
- *Julie:* Thanks for understanding and being so incredibly supportive of me, even when you didn't sign on for all that's been entailed.
- *Kelly:* Your friendship has meant the world to me! It is so wonderful to finally be able to share my joy, instead of pain!
- *Lisa:* Thanks for being so understanding, kind, and giving through everything.
- *Hemal Radia:* Thank you for inviting me in, and for allowing me to share in your positive light and energy. You made this book more than just a dream. I can never thank you enough for helping me find my way back to the light.
- *Mike Sullivan:* Thanks for sharing your advice, experience, and encouragement. It meant a lot coming from you.
- *Lori R:* Thank you for always being there when I needed you, and for the tireless work that you do 24/7. They could never possibly pay you enough!
- *Adam G:* Thank you for everything! You can't possibly know how your emails have inspired me.

- *De Boone:* It has been an honor and a pleasure to have you walking side by side with me on this journey. The advice and direction you have given me have been invaluable!
- *El and Julie Anne:* For not only being like sisters to me, but for the amazing work you do in helping others find happiness, wholeness and light. I love you both.
- *Those who share their own positive energy and light every day:* Dr. Wayne Dyer, Alan Cohen, Dr. Joe Dispenza, Dr. Lissa Rankin, and so many others! I was able to come through the adversity I faced thanks to those who led the way. Because you lit the path for me, I can now light a path for others.

PREFACE

"Don't judge me by my past. I don't live there anymore."
— Author unknown

The events you remember shape who you are today. All of the events I share in this book really happened—and they're burned into my memory. That doesn't mean there weren't many great times, as well, some of which also are included. When I look at my own life, I choose to believe there have been far more good times than bad. Some timelines are blurred, but I will do my best to put each of the events in the order in which they actually occurred. Most names have been changed to protect the identities of the individuals.

Portions of this book were *very* difficult to write, because I spent most of my life living in shame, denial, and fear that someone would discover the kind of person I really was. However, I've since learned that there is no shame in being who you are. I was a damaged girl just trying to make my way into adulthood and survive as best I could. Nobody could ever see the "damaged girl" or they would know my shame. Instead, they saw a successful, bubbly, creative overachiever.

I spent so many years worried about how other people saw me that I lost sight of who I really was. First, I was "the youngest" in the family. Later, I would become "that water ski girl." Eventually, I became "the overachiever" in my career. For half of my life, I was "that EMT," and later, "that Firefighter/EMT." Only when I was stripped of all of that, and left to stand alone, did I discover where my true strength was: in seeing the good in the world, in seeing the potential in people, in knowing that I was destined for greater things, and in learning to adapt to my new circumstances. My strength was in getting up every time I was knocked down and continuing on my path.

I now have a new respect for myself that I had never really had before. I have finally realized that each person on this earth deserves to be treated with nothing but respect! For that to happen, we must first respect ourselves. When we are able to accept our "damaged self" and integrate it with our "higher self," we become our "Divine Self." That is who we are truly meant to be!

Despite the fact that I've chosen to share my more dramatic moments and the things that I am most ashamed of, I've always had a loving family who saw only the best in me. They have been there for me every step of the way, wanting to help despite all of the years when I insisted I didn't need any help, while I secretly continued my risqué and self-destructive behavior.

I was concerned about letting my parents read the first edition of this book, because I did not want them to be hurt by the things they did not know. I did not want my family to carry the shame for the things I'd done. Instead, they digested what they did not know, opened some amazing conversations, offered me only unconditional love and acceptance, and proudly told everyone they knew about this book.

I have opened myself up to a lot of scrutiny with the hope that rape victims—and those suffering from PTSD, Depression, Fibromyalgia, or any other Invisible Illness—will see themselves in me. I hope they will realize that we are all broken in some way. Some people just hide it better. In truth, most people feel like they are living a "charade." Most people think that, if their friends and family knew who they truly were, they would be frowned upon or cast out. Even at the peak of my success, I kept waiting for someone to discover that I didn't deserve it. That was not—and never will be—the case. We all deserve to be happy. With all that I have been through, I could have chosen to wallow in self-pity. In fact, I did. *A lot!* But after being homebound and depressed for over a year, the Lord decided I needed a nudge to get out of self-pity. And through that nudge, with the assistance of my ever-loving family, I decided my house was only a possession and losing it was far less important than the love and support that they have always shown me.

I am about to take you on a journey through my life to help both you and me. There is a lesson to be learned in everything—and we continue to be taught each lesson until we learn it. Everything we experience in life either brings us closer to our true mission, teaches us a lesson, or sets us up for something far greater than we had ever dreamed. Every single event is a blessing, even if we can't see it at the time. With the right counseling, faith, and frame of mind (aka an "attitude of gratitude"), life can be whatever you decide it will be. All of us are both damaged and perfect at the same time. We all deserve to be treated with nothing but respect! To command respect from others, we must first respect ourselves, for happiness is not something to be found; it is something to become.

Bridgette

PROLOGUE

The Main Event
& the Aftermath

They say "that which does not kill you makes you stronger." As I lie here waiting to die, I know "they" are wrong. I mean, I've been through much worse than this before, and none of it killed me. Even now, I try to think of what actually "killed me." There wasn't any one major thing, just a combination of little things. I don't think I can even put it into words. And at what point does it kill me? Was it yesterday when I made the decision and wrote the note, was it today when I swallowed all three bottles of pills, or will it be in a few minutes when I fade off to sleep? I'm really not sure.

I never expected to be here. To be perfectly honest, I've always thought of depression as a character flaw rather than an illness. I've never even been able to comprehend how or why someone would choose to take his or her own life. In my 17 years as an Emergency Medical Technician, I've seen many suicide attempts. Most of them seemed to be either a cry for help or a ploy to make somebody else pay. I mean, really, if you have a bottle containing 1,000 pills and you've taken 10 of them and then call 911, am I really supposed to believe you wanted to kill yourself? I confess. I was very judgmental. I was irritated that people could do something so damned stupid. At least, that's how I used to feel—right up until the last few months.

One thing is certain: I'm getting it right. I knew which drugs to take, and I took a lot of them. I knew that if I were to fail, my problems would be so much worse than they are even now. That's why I had to wait until today. Had I done it yesterday when I really wanted to, the sheriff's department would have sent a squad to check on me when I didn't show up for work at 4:00 p.m. Today—Sunday, December 7, 2008—is the beginning of my weekend at work. Nobody is expecting me anywhere for two more days. By that time, my problems will be over and I'll no longer feel this kind of pain.

I hear my mother on the answering machine. She's begging me to pick up the phone. I can't do that. I'm already fading. If I answer the phone, she'll know. Why is she so frantic? She can't possibly know. I was very careful. Nobody knows.

I hear my next-door neighbor yelling my name. It sounds like she's in my house! I know I locked the door. Why would she pick today to use her key and come into my house? I hear her scream, "Call 911." Things start happening so quickly. I'm not sure what's going on. My friend and colleague Brad is in my face yelling, "Bridgette, it's me. It's Brad." Duh!

I know it's Brad. I just don't know why he's here. I also know that if Brad is here, then Sgt. Margo is on the way. Crap! Now everybody's going to know I'm crazy! At this point, I know I told Brad and anyone else who would listen to "get Kyle." Brad promises he will—and I believe him.

Somehow, Kyle will make this all better. He's my closest friend on the sheriff's department and one of the best people in the world. By now, I'm beyond caring that this request will only fuel the rumors that we're having an affair. Fortunately for me, Kyle's wife is a wonderful woman who's very confident in his love for her and takes the rumors in stride.

I can't comprehend how anyone who's ever met Kyle would believe for a second that he would cheat on his wife. That's not how he's built; that's one of the reasons I trust him explicitly. That's why we became friends. He is one of the few guys in the department that I trust not to have ulterior motives in befriending me. He's the rock. A former firefighter, EMT, and paratrooper, Kyle's now our firearms instructor and SWAT team leader. I just know that if anyone can fix this, Kyle can.

I know my best friend, Christine, also is here with me, but I'm not sure how or why. (I have a vague recollection of leaving her a voicemail saying I am sorry, but I knew she was on a conference call and wouldn't get it until after I was gone.) I see the EMTs from the local rescue squad, many of whom I've known for years. They are also telling me I know them. After this, I remember nothing.

I opened my eyes and saw a blue wall. As I tried to figure out where I was, I realized that a tube was down my throat and that I wasn't breathing on my own. It all came rushing back. I thought to myself, "Son of a bitch. I'm still here!" As I looked around, I saw my mother on one side of my bed holding my hand, Christine on the other, and my father and three of my brothers sitting against the wall. They were all crying. "What the hell?" It never occurred to me that people would actually care if I were gone. Why didn't it occur to me? I've always known how much my family loves me. Why was I so certain that they would all be better off without me? How could I possibly have done this to them? It had made such perfect sense for a week. For the last few weeks, or even months, suicide had seemed like a perfectly logical option. It felt like the right thing to do. I would no longer be a burden on anyone, and I would be at peace. Now, I can't even imagine what I was thinking; and yet, a part of me still wished I would just drift back off to sleep and not wake up again.

I had no sense of day or time. I'm not sure if I had been asleep for hours, days, or weeks. I tried to speak, but I couldn't. I tried to make hand gestures and realized my hands were tied down. I was coherent enough to know that I was on a ventilator and couldn't pull the tube out, but it gagged me and I needed to move it a little to the right.

Unfortunately, everyone assumed I was trying to pull it out and they jumped up to secure me more than I already was. It turned into a struggle. I was gagging! Suddenly I vomited. It was something I'd seen a thousand times and could gladly go without ever seeing again: activated charcoal. It was a horrible sight. Black goo. I remembered seeing patients in the E.R. being forced to drink charcoal. I always thought it was a fitting punishment for doing such a stupid thing. Now, I was the one who had done that stupid thing! Fortunately for me, before I even had to think about being cleaned up and changed, everything went black again.

I came to again and tried to ask what day it is. My family understood and told me it's Monday. Good. I've only been here one day. My doctor came in the room to see me. I wanted to crack a joke (my typical response to anything remotely uncomfortable), but I couldn't speak. I asked for paper and a pen. I tried to write words, but it just looked like scribbles. Why couldn't I write? I tried again, but it just came out as scribbles again. I had been trying to say, "It looks like we'll need to change my anti-depressants." I thought it was funny at the time, but I couldn't manage to write it. Looking back, it wasn't all that funny. Oh, well. My doctor didn't bother to wait anyway.

My family told me a little about the chain of events that had occurred the night before. They talked to me, even though I couldn't respond. My Aunt Sandy walked up to my bedside and told me, "If you ever do something so stupid again, I'll kill you myself." I'm told that my eyes got as big as saucers. Mom told me that Kyle had come to the hospital and sat in the E.R. with me; she had left the room for a bit and he was there when she returned. She immediately said, "You must be Kyle. Thank you for being here for my daughter." Later, he would tell me that he had been feeling uncomfortable and out of place, but when my mother acknowledged who he was and thanked him, he felt much better.

The next thing I knew was that I would be taken downstairs to the "Mental Health Unit" on Tuesday afternoon. I was on a Chapter 51 Emergency Detention. This wasn't possible. Only crazy people get chaptered—and I was *not* one of them! As they wheeled me down the hall, I was sobbing. I begged my family to just let me go home. Although the practical me knew it wasn't possible, the desperate me wanted to believe we could all just pretend this never happened. "I'm not really crazy. It was just temporary insanity! Can't I have a do over?"

I was downstairs lying on a cold, hard bed in the psych ward. Alone. Crying. I didn't want to be here! I wanted to go home. The staff came and told me that I was required to attend the "group session." Like I really wanted to go and talk to a bunch of crazy people! Didn't they realize I just got here? Couldn't they just leave me alone?

How would I explain to anyone why I am here? I didn't even understand it. My life hadn't been all that traumatic. In fact, compared to most people, my life had been *really* good!

PART 1

Discovery & Connection

"Far away there in the sunshine are my highest aspirations.
I may not reach them, but I can look up and
see their beauty, believe in them,
and try to follow where they lead." ~ **Louisa May Alcott**

chapter 1

The Water Bug

*A*s I dragged the water skis from the porch down to the beach, one by one, I wished everyone would hurry up. We only had a few weeks to ski, and I couldn't wait! Every July, my family rented a cottage for two weeks in July—that included my birthday—and then for another week in August. My brothers carried me in their arms as we skied around the lake. Then we progressed to doing tricks. Today was my big day! It was the first day I would get to ski behind the boat by myself. I was a big girl! I had just turned 5. I was afraid of the boat before, so I had learned to ski with my father, who helped me at the end of the dock while my four brothers held the other end of the rope and ran up the shore pulling me to safety. I'd gotten pretty good at that. *Finally!* The sun rose, and my dad and my brothers joined me down on the beach. Dad drove the boat while one of my brothers helped me in the water. I was *so* scared. I mean, if I fell, I'd be all alone in that big lake! It took a couple of tries, but I got up and skied in a big circle around the lake. It was so much fun! It hadn't occurred to me that my mother should have seen this huge event. I just knew she would be in the cottage, cooking, cleaning, or lying in front of a fan. Mom wasn't really a water person. During the weeks when we were at the cottage, she spent a lot of time in the kitchen preparing fresh snacks and delicious homemade meals.

Fast forward to the following May. I wasn't just scared, but terrified! I sat on a freezing dock with a stranger behind the wheel of a ski boat. My brother John stood next to me, offering last-minute instructions. If all went right, the stranger (who said his name was Mark) would pull me off of the dock and I'd ski a small circle. John held the rope as the loops fed out further and further until there were no more loops and the boat pulled me off of the dock. *I did it!* I was officially a member of the Water Bugs Ski Team. Of course, I was still 5, so I didn't really know what that meant, but I was in.

I spent that first summer learning to ski while standing on other people, instead of on my own skis. By mid-summer, our Junior Doubles act was a big hit. A boy of about 13 and I did three different tricks—including me standing on his thighs while waving to the crowd, lying back over his shoulders held by only one foot, and finally locking my legs around his waist taking the rope, and lying back to hold both of us while he waved to the crowd. We were even pictured in *Water Ski Magazine!* My other big act in the show was the Junior Pyramid. I enjoyed all of the attention, but I *hated* being so cold. Because I was the youngest member of the team, I received a lot of attention from the older skiers. They all treated me like I was their own child. I didn't want to be a child. I was one of them. I wanted to be treated like a skier, not a child.

Late June arrived and I quickly realized that I had yet to learn the true meaning of the word "cold." The Water Bugs team had an annual contract to ski at Milwaukee's Summerfest, the largest music festival in the world, located on Lake Michigan. The waves were as big as I was, and the water was freezing cold. The course we skied was a half mile each way. The first time I fell in the water, I was so shocked by the cold that it took me a minute to catch my breath. The nice thing was that, if I fell, one of the guys was required to let go and stay with me. Fortunately, I didn't fall often—not because I was skilled, but because I was so small. Someone was always able to grab me, and put me on their own skis. I would then climb to their shoulders.

The downside to having a summer sport was that my classmates never knew I was really good at something—and I didn't have time during the summer for bonding and play dates. I always wondered if that's why I didn't have any close friends during my first six years of school. When I was home to play, I always spent time with the neighborhood kids. I had a best friend in kindergarten, but she moved away before first grade. My best friend in first grade moved away before second grade. I didn't have any close friends after that, and I was very self-conscious about that.

Up until about the third grade, I thought there were only two religions in the world: Catholic and Public. That's because all of the kids in the neighborhood either went to Catholic school or public school. I went to a K-8 Catholic school. It's been a lifelong joke that one of my friends invited me to a movie night at her school, and I said, "I'm not sure if I can go there. I'm not public, I'm Catholic."

One day while sitting at my desk in school, I figured out that other kids in my class actually spent time together away from school. I couldn't figure out how they did that. I felt very isolated. All of my neighborhood friends were either a grade ahead of me, or a grade behind me. At recess, we were able to play together, but then we had to go back to our separate classes.

Our school had uniforms, and I hated dress-up days. Most of my clothes were hand-me-down clothes from my older brothers. I knew we didn't have much money, so I tried not to ask for much. In February one year, our school had a "Valentine's Day dress-up day." Students were expected to wear red and white, and those who showed up in uniform, were ridiculed. I dreaded that day. The problem was, I didn't have any red-and-white clothes. I did *not* want to go to school. I don't remember ever mentioning it to my parents. One day, my mom took me shopping with her. We weren't there to buy anything for me. She made that very clear on the way over to the store. Once there, I saw the most amazing dress! It was white with red strawberries on it, and it had a little red jacket. I asked and begged and asked and begged, but Mom just kept saying we couldn't afford it. I tried to understand, but I was devastated.

Valentine's Day arrived, and Mom came in my room to wake me for school. I told her I wasn't going to school that day. When she asked why, I said it was because I had nothing to wear, and kids would make fun of me. She said, "Why don't you wear this?" I rolled over to see that she was holding up *the* dress. I don't think I ever got out of bed faster! I was so proud wearing my new dress to school that day—and to any other occasion I could think of after that. It was truly amazing how one piece of clothing could transform the way I felt about myself!

I wore that dress to the dinner-dance at the Annual Water Ski Show

Convention, and I danced all night with my family and some of the other young skiers. I still have a picture from that night, and you can see how happy and proud I was. As long as I had my dress on, nobody would even think to make fun of me! I was still young enough to be considered "cute," and was absolutely doted upon by my four brothers, my parents, and the other members of my ski-team. I loved that convention. My fellow Water Bugs were anxious to demonstrate to the other teams how well this "little skier" had learned to ski. They even arranged for me to ski across the hotel pool. Once again, I was the center of attention. I really liked that feeling.

chapter 2

Finally, Real friends!

Up until the fifth grade, during recess I continued to hang out with friends from the neighborhood. Then, recess times were changed and I had to make friends with kids my own age. One day, I sat on the window sill in the girls' bathroom avoiding class when a girl named Jane came up to me. She asked if I wanted to "do something" after school. I had no idea what "do something" meant, but I said yes. We went to the local community center and played games with another friend of hers named Lana. From that day on, the three of us were inseparable. We spent a lot of time at the community center playing bumper pool or air hockey. We took music lessons together, had a lot of sleepovers, and we focused on a mutual goal: the end of fifth grade was when you could finally try out for cheerleading. The squads were in sixth, seventh, and eighth grades, and tryouts began at the end of the fifth grade year. Our school had won the state cheerleading championships for many years in a row, so the pressure was on. The three of us practiced for months and months. Finally, the big day came. I was nervous, but confident. I had been waiting for this day for *years*.

The typical squad had nine "regular" cheerleaders and one alternate. When the scores were announced, I qualified in the number nine spot. However, the rules for selecting our squad suddenly changed. Only eight cheerleaders and two alternates were chosen. Deep down, I knew this decision was because they didn't want me as a regular. I took solace in at least being an alternate with my best friend, Jane, who scored five points below me. What I didn't foresee was that practice took place during the summer, which meant I had to miss a *lot* of practice because I was always skiing at either a show, individual tournament, or training.

That summer, I practiced skiing a *lot*. My brother John took me out on the water at every opportunity. He even entered me in the Wisconsin State Three Event Tournament. The three events were trick skiing, jumping, and slalom. What he couldn't teach me, I learned from coaches brought in by John. At one point, I slept at my brother's house for an entire week so I could continue training. John had just recently purchased a lake home where he and his fiancée, Sandy, were to live after their wedding that fall. He hired a boat driver who would come to wake me up early in the morning. He had instructions from John as to what I should be working on, and when. I skied from early morning until lunch, stopped to eat, and then hit the water again. I stayed out until dinner time, when John would come home from work. We ate dinner together, and then we'd go back out onto the lake so I could show him what I'd learned that day. As the state tournament approached, we were working at a frenzied pace so I could learn as many tricks as possible. One day while practicing with a trick skiing coach, I fell and was hit in the back of the head by the trick ski. I complained about it when the boat came back around. John said I would be fine, and I put my hands against the boat waiting to hear why I had fallen. (In all honesty, John had good reason to say I was fine. I complained a lot, especially during jumping practice.) I said to him, "If I'm so fine, why is blood running down the side of the boat?" He looked and saw what I saw. We were done for the day. He packed me up and took me home to Mom, who was a nurse. She thought I needed stitches, so she called our family doctor. I was driven to the clinic, where he stitched up my head and told my family to keep me out of the lake for a while. The tournament was in less than a week! I didn't practice again until the night before. I felt such incredible pressure to make John and everyone else proud and happy—so much so that I thought I might vomit. I've always wondered how child athletes, such as young gymnasts preparing for the Olympics, manage all the stress between the ages of 8 and 12! The tournament was a five-hour drive from where we lived, and I rode up with John and Dad. We shared a hotel room with one of my trick coaches and his friend; they were also competing in their own divisions. I don't recall if Mom was sick or working, but she had a very bad back, and riding five hours in a car wouldn't have done her much good.

In trick skiing, participants are scored on the total point value of each trick performed during two 20-second passes. I was on the last trick of my second pass when I fell. I wasn't sure if I'd done enough for the win. Then, I looked up to see my brother, Dad, coaches, and teammates standing at the end of the dock jumping up and down. That was when I knew I'd won. I was walking on air for the next few days. That year, I took the gold medal in trick skiing and bronze in slalom. I was not eligible for the all-around title because I could not jump. Despite many exasperating attempts by my brother John to teach me, I simply couldn't help but avoid the jump on every run. Fortunately, the joy of my trick-skiing title far outshone the fact that I didn't jump. We even stopped to play at a water park on the drive home! Everyone on the ski team, my family, and my friends were really happy for me, and impressed by my trick skiing victory. The icing on the cake was that I earned my first "trio" act in the show. As one girl jumped and another slalomed, I did trick skiing at the same time. It was *really* special.

Unfortunately, one day as we prepared for this act in the show, I just knew we would not be skiing. It was one of my most horrific memories, and it probably played a major role in determining my eventual career path.

Just as we were about to ski our "Junior Three-Event" act, my brother Joe was performing an act on a slalom ski in which he would "crack the whip," just as the boat made what is called a "power turn." The boat would suddenly turn and stop in its tracks. Joe then would ski all the way around the boat, and then the boat would continue on as Joe completed one more trick on the show course. On this particular day, a disabled boat sat on the outer edge of the show course. Once Joe began his cut, he could hit speeds as high as 60 mph. This particular night, the disabled boat just happened to be in the path where Joe hit his highest speed. He saw it with a split second to spare and threw himself onto his back. The sound of Joe hitting that boat was horrific! I tried to run towards…well, I don't even know where…when someone grabbed me by the arm and said, "See? He's waving. He's okay." (The first thing a show skier is taught is to always wave when you fall to notify drivers and safety personnel that you are fine.) I remember thinking, "There is *no way* he is okay." The show was stopped at that point. I ran to the dock as the safety boat brought Joe in. He was bleeding profusely from both feet, and I would swear I saw a bone sticking out! My dad was standing on the end of the dock when Joe said, "Get Mom." In a perfect example of my family's dark sense of humor, my father said, "What do you think? Your mother's a miracle worker? You don't need your mother, you need a surgeon!"

People held towels on Joe's feet and legs until the ambulance arrived. I will never forget how helpless I felt in that moment. I wanted to do something to ease his pain and stop the bleeding. I don't remember packing my bags or changing my clothes, but I rode with Mom and Dad to the hospital. While we were in the waiting room of the E.R., my mother received a call from the emergency room of another hospital. It turned out my brother John also had been hurt in the boat introduction of the show. He dislocated his shoulder when a bolt broke on his seat just as he had been doing a "power turn." I had two brothers in two different hospitals. Between the three of us skiers, there would be many more E.R. visits over the years! On this night, I was overjoyed to learn that only one of Joe's feet was broken and the bleeding had been stopped. He was even going to be released from the hospital that same night!

My joy turned to absolute misery when I arrived at the next cheerleading practice and discovered that they'd made Jane a "regular." I was now the only alternate. I had suspected this was the plan all along, but I still couldn't believe they had done it. I liked to believe in the good in people, especially those in authority at a Catholic school. I lost all respect for my coach, but I continued to push to be the best I could be, for my friends. I also began to resent my brother John for pushing me to ski the individual tournaments, thus costing me that spot on the squad. I loved skiing in the shows, but I couldn't care less about individual tournaments. Now they had cost me the one thing that I really wanted.

Throughout the sixth grade, I sat on the sidelines while the squad performed the half-time routine, and competed in tournaments. On the very rare occasion when someone was gone, I was there to take her place.

It was really difficult to remember nine different parts (the challenge of being an alternate), and if I got anything wrong, everyone made sure I knew it. But at least I got to wear the uniform and cheer on the sidelines during basketball games.

Who am I kidding? I still felt like a loser.

The following summer was filled with more water skiing, and that year John was determined to help me win the all-around title—if only I could jump. He sent me to a couple ski schools. In early June, I went to one school way "up north." A couple of the other girls from my ski team went, as well. As usual, I was the youngest person there, so nobody really talked to me. I hated being there. Even the girls and women from my own ski team ignored or dismissed me as a child, even those who were only two years older than me. The instructors would get us up very early, and even with a full-length wetsuit, the water was freezing. My wetsuit never had a chance to fully dry in the cold Wisconsin nights, so putting it on in the morning wasn't exactly a lot of fun. Some of the older kids told me there were leeches in this lake! I hated the thought of that, because leeches terrified me!

No coach could figure out why I couldn't land a jump and ski away. They kept saying my form was perfect. The answer was very simple; I didn't want to. When approaching a six-foot ramp at about twenty miles per hour, it looked like a brick wall. I was only 10 years old. I don't ever remember a time when my knees didn't hurt; the landing from that ramp didn't help.

I kept to myself that week. I was jealous of all of the attention the older girls were getting. I received a call from home that my first niece had been born on June 9. I was so excited, and yet so sad. I was stuck far away, all alone, and I couldn't hold her. I enjoyed going to the gym, which was solitary and quiet. I tried to enjoy the balance beam, using it for cartwheels and pretending I was a "real" gymnast. I would spend the next seven years or more thinking of that beautiful niece as the center of my world.

When the state tournament came around again, I was unaware of the drama that had been unfolding behind the scenes. I had driven up to the site of the tournament with the family that ran the ski school where I spent most of my time. We were running late. When we arrived and pulled into the parking lot, John and one of my trick coaches met us at the van. My name had been called to report to the dock for the jumping event, and I was just about out of time. John picked me up, and the coach grabbed my jumping equipment. They ran with me and my gear as fast as they could go, for about 200 yards to the dock, where they were calling my name. (They didn't want me running, or I might be winded for the event.)

I had finally learned to jump that summer, thanks to Mark, that first boat driver that I'd had from the age of 5. Either the coach from the ski school or John must have called him. He could always calm me down. He came out to the house operated by the school and said, "Okay, you and I will just go out on a pair of jumpers, and we'll jump the wakes. If at any time you decide you want to go over the ramp, let me know and we'll do it." I had never seen Mark behind the boat. He was always the driver. I trusted him behind the wheel of a boat more than I trusted anyone. He never let me down. That day, he was a skier rather than a driver as he went out wake jumping with me. He left the decision in my hands, and that took away the fear. And so, when my brother sat me down on the dock at the state tournament after nearly arriving too late, I was ready to jump. I stripped down to my swimsuit, put on my vest and jump shorts, and then used shampoo to get the jumpers on my feet (the bindings were *that* tight). I sat down on the dock and waited…and waited…and waited. I was so nervous! I was singing a song to calm myself down. All I remember is that the chorus went "round and round." I thought it was appropriate, because that's what my stomach was doing. I landed my first jump, which was a huge relief. Now I was at least eligible for the all-around title. There was still a lot of work to do to improve my jumping. I was trying to get more distance, because that's what you are scored on. In the Junior Girls Division (under 12), only three of us were doing ski jumping. I'd been taught how to cut towards the ramp as late as possible, "pop" at the top of the ramp and lean out over my skis. I'd conquered my fear of the ramp, but not my fear of a horrific landing. I'm certain that my cut and "pop" didn't look like gold to anyone who knew about jumping, but I knew I'd done the best I could. That summer I won the trick title again and took third in slalom and in jumping. I was disappointed not to win the all-around, but I was happy that it was over—and I had conquered the ramp.

After sixth grade, one of the "regular" cheerleaders moved away. That moved me in as a "regular," and there was a new alternate. It was so much easier to do a routine when you only had to remember one part! Seventh grade went smoothly. I believe our squad won state again.

Jane, Lana and I spent almost all of our time together. We slept over at one another's houses at least two to four nights a week. We did homework together, took music lessons together, and did "normal" seventh grader things. In addition to cheerleading, we also joined the track team, the basketball team, and we continued on the soccer team, which my brother Ryan had coached since I had been in the fourth grade. At least one day a week, we practiced track on the playground right after school, walked to the community center for cheerleading practice, had a parent pick us up and feed us, and then were taken to a gym for basketball practice. In all honesty, I was not good at basketball and couldn't run worth a damn, which made track and soccer unlikely places to excel. Even with my own brother as coach, I still failed at soccer, playing an average of two minutes a game. At least in track, I learned to throw a shot put that could beat out almost any other girl.

If only these people could see me ski, they would at least know I excelled at *something!*

Jane, Lana, and I had three additional close friends who rounded out our "group." One of them was Loraine. She and I would share a daily babysitting job in the eighth grade and stay very close through high school and beyond. By now, I was aware of the "social order of grade school," and I fell at the very bottom of the top, meaning I hung out with the "popular girls," but was the least popular of the group. It is funny now how acutely aware of my social standing I was, and how I was very self-conscious about it, despite the fact that I still had great friends.

chapter 3

Switching to Shows

*I*n the summer between seventh and eighth grade, my brother John was planning his wedding to Sandy, so there was no longer any pressure to ski the individual tournaments. I was relieved to turn my attention to show skiing. I wanted to be the "Star Swivel Skier" in the show since I'd first gotten my Swivel Ski a couple of years earlier. Swivel was relatively new at that time, and all female skiers were being encouraged to learn to do it. Swivel skiing is much like ballet on the water. The binding of the ski is mounted on ball bearings that can be set to turn 180 or 360 degrees, and that allows the skier to do different turns, tricks, and spins.

Despite the fact that by now I'd been a member of the team for close to seven years, I never felt like I fit in. I always thought it was my age, but as I got older, new girls only a year or two older than me joined the team and seemed to be accepted right away. Nobody ever really talked to me; they talked over me. I felt like they still saw me as a 5-year-old girl or just as "Joe's little sister." By the time I was 12, I no longer was the youngest skier. I also had developed a major weight complex, because I was never selected for the "doubles" show acts—involving a man and a woman doing different lifts on the water—or upper level of the pyramids. I was surrounded every day by bikini-clad women with hip bones sticking out! I now realize that I would never have had time to be in doubles, or a part of most pyramids, because I was always going right from one act to the next. People were literally waiting to help me change costumes, and hand me my equipment so that I could head right back onto the dock. Nonetheless,

I felt neglected at a time when all I wanted was to stand out and feel good about myself, by being the best and most versatile skier.

Before long, I figured out that there were a couple of tricks on a swivel ski that, once learned, could be used as a base for more difficult tricks. The "flip turn" has the skier hold the rope out in front with one hand while turning at the hips and skiing backwards. Once I mastered this trick, I wrapped the handle behind my back, holding just the rope in front of me. As I turned, I brought the handle from around my back out over my head. It was an impressive-looking trick, but it was actually the same trick, just with more flash. By putting my back foot on the rope, I was able to release my back hand so that both hands were now over my head while I held an arched pose skiing backwards. This was always a crowd-pleaser. I practiced at home all winter. I had purchased an elastic type of surgical tubing that clipped around any beam, pole, or doorknob. I attached my own handle to the tubing. I took the tubing and my swivel ski everywhere I would go— even to babysit—or used it in my basement at home. When I practiced on land, my ski was always set to turn 360 degrees, so that I got used to the balancing act of not having anything to stop my turns but me. I worked on basic tricks, as well as some of the more difficult turns, including one in which the rope was pulled up over your head while turning a complete circle. I learned that by extending my free leg behind me at the start of the turn and then sweeping it up and around as I turned, it looked far more graceful, and more difficult, than it actually was. By the summer of 1985, I was the "Star Swivel Skier!" It felt amazing! I got to pick my own music and costume. I was the center of attention! This was *huge*, because most of the time I felt invisible.

My brother Joe, who is nine years older than me, still lived at home, and he was also on the team. He took me with him to every practice and show. Afterward, he would take me out to the bar with him. Because I was so much younger than everyone there, not many people even noticed me. I was only 12 years old and in a bar two to three nights a week, just drinking soda and talking to no one. I wanted to be like the older women on the team who got constant attention. Later, as an adult, I knew that the kind of attention those women got wasn't the kind of attention I deserved at my age.

Millions of people want to be the center of attention and are just afraid to admit it. As they grow up, they tend to either be Type-A, high-performing employees, and creative entrepreneurs, or the trashy dressing women who seek out the wrong kind of attention. After two years of therapy, and a best friend who constantly told me that it isn't a bad thing to want attention, I was finally able to admit that I had always wanted to be the center of attention—and I particularly wanted the attention of men. I never understood why, because in my family I certainly was the center of attention! I had a Dad and four brothers who completely doted on me. Why did I need to catch a boy's attention or a man's attention to make me feel validated as a person when I had plenty of that at home? In therapy, a couple years after my suicide attempt, my Therapist suggested that I had missed out on a "normal mother-daughter relationship." Because she was often ill, going to school, or working, my Mom and I had spent little time together, having conversations that most mothers and daughters have. I didn't realize I had missed anything, because I kept so busy with my Dad and brothers.

Once the suggestion was made, I tried to remember mother-daughter time and could only pull out a few memories. I remembered the summer between seventh and eighth grade when my jaw dropped as my mom told me she was taking me back-to-school shopping for new clothes. I couldn't believe it! It was an amazing trip for me. We bought a ton of shirts, sweaters, and pants. I got to pick out what I liked. When I found a shirt that I really liked but couldn't decide on a color, she said, "We'll get them both." I felt like I'd just won the lottery! The shopping trip had cost about $150, and I couldn't believe my mother was spending so much money on *me!* I don't know where she got it, but it was so wonderful.

While therapists seemed to place blame for many misgivings on parents, I considered myself lucky to have two of the most supportive, kind, and loving parents in the world. We may not have had a typical mother-daughter relationship when I was growing up, but it blossomed into a most wonderful one. My mom is one of my best friends, and I look forward to talking to her every day. My mom was—and still is—the biggest supporter of this book, *Fallen Angel Rising*, despite all that she had to learn about her daughter. After recovering from the initial shock of all that she had read, she not only embraced the book, but she continued loving me unconditionally and without judgment. This project has fostered some of the most honest and wonderful conversations between us. She is proud of me, and takes this book everywhere she goes. I am truly blessed!

It should also be noted that, before I was ever conceived, five pathologists diagnosed my mother with a rare, terminal liver disease. She was told to abort me, because she did not have more than a year to live. She refused. Throughout most of my childhood, my mother believed she was dying. Every time she got sick, she thought it was the end. And despite that, she continued working to help support our family. She often picked up extra shifts as a pool nurse after my father was laid off from his job.

By the time eighth grade arrived, I was settled into my place in life. The cheerleading season was going incredibly well. Our routine was out of this world, and there was no way we wouldn't win state. But, as usual, I still had the conflict between cheerleading and skiing. The annual Water Ski Convention took place the same weekend as the State Cheerleading Competition. I went to the convention on Friday and Saturday night and would be home early enough on Sunday to compete in cheerleading. However, that convention would prove to be one of the worst experiences of my life.

chapter 4

You Can't Make This Stuff Up!

By now my parents no longer attended the water-ski conventions. My brother Joe always arranged for me to have a hotel room with some of the younger girls on my team. This year, most of them either weren't there, or had made other arrangements. I was rooming with a woman whom I had met a few times. She skied for another team, and I was pretty sure Joe had a thing for her.

There were twin girls, just two years older than me, who were known in the trick-skiing world as "prodigies." The number of difficult tricks they could do in 20 seconds was mind-boggling. Fortunately, due to our age difference, I never had to compete against them. At this conference, I ended up hanging around with the twins on the night of the dance. They lived in the city where the convention was being held. Their father, who was known to be strict, wanted to leave the event. They begged him to stay, so I told him that the twins could stay in my room, and that I would stay with them. When I make a promise, it's important to me. Despite the fact that the twins were two years older than me, I sensed they were more sheltered and that I was the "street smart" one.

Later that evening, we all began to hang out with a boy I knew from another ski team. Mike, 14, was a year older than me. Mike told us he had to be back in his room by a certain time, but we could all come. The twins were determined to go, and so we went. They lay in one bed with Mike, while I dozed off in the other bed. A short time later, Mike's 18-year-old brother came back to the room. He and I decided to leave the room and go for a walk. We wandered the halls looking for good parties. (Yes. You read that right. At 13 years old, I was wandering the halls of a hotel at around 2:00 a.m. looking for "good parties.") Not much was happening, so we returned to the room. He stripped down to his underwear and crawled into bed. I was fully dressed and on top of the covers. I won't deny that he was beautiful. I would have loved for him to kiss me, but I wouldn't have known what to do after that. Nothing happened. We both fell asleep. I kept waking up and telling the twins that we had to go back to the room. They kept saying "just a few more minutes," and I kept falling back to sleep. I should have either been more forceful or just left them there, but I had made a promise to their father and I intended to keep it. I was so tired and couldn't stay awake.

Before I knew it, it was 4:00 a.m. Someone knocked on the door. Mike got up to answer it. He opened the door and I heard him say, "You can't come in." I heard the ominous voice of my brother Joe asking, "Why not?" Mike said, "I have girls in here." Before I knew it, Joe walked into the room, right past the bed where I was lying. I stood up against the wall. When he turned and saw me, he threw his full beer at me, hitting me in the chest while simultaneously cussing. I tried to explain to him that nothing happened, that I'd promised the twins' father I would stay with them. We took our "discussion" into the hallway. I had a shirt covered in beer and we were arguing. He is nine years older than I am, so you can imagine how this looked to a stranger. At that moment, the wrong stranger came along. He was a short man who looked like he kept the steroid industry in business. He was also *very* drunk. When he saw the scene we made, he started beating on my brother.

I knew that a group of large guys from my ski team were partying just past the next fire door. I ran to get them and said, "Come quick! Some guy is beating the crap out of my brother!" About that time, my brother stumbled through the fire door with the body builder on his back. One of my teammates jumped on the body builder to pull him off of Joe, and then someone jumped on him. Mike's older brother then appeared. He calmly stepped out of his hotel room, grabbed the guy by the throat and held him up against the wall with his feet dangling off the floor. He calmly said, "Is there a problem here?" When everyone finally settled down and the story was explained, the man was terribly sorry for beating on my brother. I guess they had a few beers together that weekend—and at conventions to come.

I went back to Mike's room and ordered the twins to get back to our room. They *still* wanted to stay. With all of the anger and frustration I was feeling, I said, "I promised your father you would sleep in my room, and that is where you will stay." They realized I wasn't joking. They returned to my room, where we all went to sleep. They were gone when I woke up. I was devastated—not because I'd just been used, had my life destroyed, and was abandoned by two of the most famous skiers in the world without even a "thank you," "I'm sorry," or "here's some money for the room," but because I *knew* that Joe didn't believe me when I told him nothing happened. That was the most horrific thing I could think of. I spent three to four nights a week with this amazing brother, who drove me to and from ski practice and shows, and even took me to the bar with him afterwards. He took me on long-distance road trips for tournaments, and pro tour events, too. Not too many big brothers would drag their little sister around everywhere, but he always did so without any complaints. Now he had every reason not to trust me. I felt like I had betrayed him, and I felt awful. I never brought it up again, because I assumed he'd never believe me, no matter what I said. Even though I knew I'd done nothing wrong, I felt like I should have just left the twins behind, or dragged their selfish, spoiled, and entitled little asses out by the hair.

chapter 5

Not Exactly Feeling Cheerful

I didn't sleep much that night, or the next, so I showed up tired for State Cheerleading Competition. I don't know what I told my friends or the coach. I was just ready to get through the competition and then go home to crash. Despite our amazing routine, we didn't win state that year. I never knew why, but I've often wondered if it was something I did. You lose points if someone isn't smiling for even a second. I hope it wasn't me, but if it was I guess it was karma for the coach, who'd screwed me over to begin with by not making me a regular cheerleader. I still felt so bad about Joe that I didn't sleep for weeks.

Our cheerleading squad went to another competition that year—a High School Regional Tournament in Peoria, Illinois—and the top squads would advance to Orlando for Nationals. Despite being only in the eighth grade, somehow we qualified to compete against the best high schools in the region. We took several cars and vans for the five-hour trip and got to stay in a hotel. When it was our turn to perform, just about everything that could go wrong did. Pyramids fell, lifts didn't work, and our routine was a disaster. I felt bad, but frankly, all I could really think was, "Thank God it wasn't me!"

All things come to an end, and so did the eighth grade and graduation from the Catholic school. It was a difficult goodbye, because most of us had been in the same class since kindergarten. We had become very close as a class—not just a lot of separate cliques. In hindsight, it was almost comical how many tears were shed over leaving eighth grade, when, in fact, most of us would be going to the same high school. Many of us stayed within a 60-mile radius for most of our lives. It wasn't as if we wouldn't see each other again. There was one exception. Kurt, one of our favorite boys in the class, and his older brother Craig were moving to Cincinnati. Many of us also had become very fond of their little sister in the first grade. We had many fun nights sneaking out of Lana's house during sleepovers to throw rocks at Kurt's window. In fact, between fifth and sixth grade, Jane, Lana, and I would play "Truth or Dare" with Kurt, and another boy from our class named Donny. Donny was the first boy I French kissed as a result of the game—and I liked it. Donny and I had known each other since before kindergarten. Our parents were good friends, and we lived only four blocks from each other. I have many fond memories of my childhood with Donny, including the summer he taught me to play "quarters," using soda instead of beer, during our annual "Family Camp" trip that our parents and friends took us on every year. Ironically, I had four brothers who were much older than I was, and Donny had four sisters who were about the same ages as my brothers.

chapter 6

Welcome to High School

While most of my classmates were terrified to go to high school, I had no fear. I was going to an all-girls school, and almost all of my friends were, too. It was nice to start something new surrounded by friends. Another high school nearby was just for boys. It was the best of both worlds: without boys in my school, we didn't have to worry about making an ass of ourselves during the day if we'd slept late or said something stupid; and we enjoyed the same social activities as a co-ed school, like football and basketball games. At first, I hung out with my grade school friends and the new friends they had made—the popular group. We'd go to football games together, and spend time at one another's houses. Then one day, I had an epiphany. It was just too hard to be friends with these people. I was trying too hard, and losing myself in the process. By then I had made other friends and developed other interests. I decided that friendship wasn't supposed to be hard work.

Early in my freshman year, I was scheduled to have surgery on both knees. Waterskiing was beginning to take its toll. We scheduled the surgery for fall so that I could recover in time for the next season. The surgery left school sports out of the question. I was used to performing for a crowd—I could sing and act pretty well—so I decided to try out for the musical at the boy's school with my grade school friend Loraine. We were both cast in the chorus. Every day after school we would trek through the woods to the boy's school for play practice. We had a lot of fun, especially when we weren't on stage. We played hide-and-seek in the auditorium and watched

TV in the dressing rooms. We also met a lot of great people who became great friends.

I met my first official "boyfriend," Peter, during that first musical. He was the stage manager and built all of the sets. He could run around on the catwalks and hang by light cords as if he were only four feet off the ground. It always scared me a little bit, but I went up there to conquer my fear. I liked it. He could also play piano like nobody I'd ever heard before. To this day, I can remember and play part of a song he wrote. It was beautiful. When I had knee surgery, he sent me roses and a card signed by everyone. It was sweet—but suffocating.

Although he was good to me, Peter and I were just not meant to be. I was a freshman and he was a senior. I was outgoing and he was introverted. I liked to be the center of attention and he stayed behind the scenes. Most of all, I was a freshman in high school and there was so much more to experience. I didn't want to be tied down right away—so we broke up. Peter was still interested in me, and I felt bad for hurting him, right up until 25 years later when we reconnected on Facebook, and his true colors came out. More on that later.

I was up and running not too long after surgery. I was between plays, so I asked the track coach for approval to work out with his team in the weight room after school. He said yes. For the first time, I became aware of my physical strength. One day, as I was bench-pressing, the coach began to add weight. The more weight he added, the more people stopped what they were doing to watch. Pretty soon, the whole gym was silent while everyone watched me lift. I began to get self-conscious and waiver a bit. I honestly don't know how much weight I benched that day, but it was enough to give me a reputation. People became afraid of me! I'd never been in a fight in my life, and now just the idea of it had people being very nice to me. (I guess all those years of waterskiing had done wonders for my chest, shoulders, and back. That would explain why I could never find a dress with sleeves that fit!)

I had a very small role in the spring musical and the fall drama at the boys' school. After those experiences, I felt I was more talented than some of the people being cast, so I moved into drama at my girls' school. I was immediately given a lead role and would continue to have lead roles for the rest of my high school career. It was not only fun, but it gave me freedom not enjoyed by anyone else in the school. I had a permanent hall pass to get me out of any study hall so I could go to the auditorium, where we had set up a love seat, chair, and TV in the Teacher/Director's Office. My friends and I met there every day. Some days, I would actually get some homework done; most days, we just goofed off. I remember trying out a new fog machine in that small office. We closed the door and turned on the machine until you couldn't even see your hand in front of your face. It was really funny, in a "you had to be there" sort of way. I learned to navigate the catwalks and manage all of the lights and sound systems in the auditorium. This gave me another free pass for all school assemblies. I got to hang out in the balcony with my friends instead of with my class.

I haven't mentioned much about getting homework done, because I never really did get it done. In whatever class I was sitting in, I was usually trying to complete assignments for the next class. And then there was the infamous "homework caper." To complete a creative writing assignment, we were supposed to use our free periods to go to the library and use reference cards. I never went to the library. The night before the homework was due, I went with my friend Stacey from play practice, and we broke into the library. We took the cards, went home, did the assignment, and got to school early the next morning to return the cards. Knowledge of our escapade spread among our theater friends and even a few teachers. After that, I even fielded a few requests from staff to break into certain classrooms or storage areas to get something they needed. Fortunately, the school was more than a hundred years old, so I was usually up to the task. I managed to do well in school without preparing much because I was able to pass almost any test on material I had heard. If the teacher lectured on it, I was listening. My theory was: "Why read the book when she just told us everything about it?" I never figured out why teachers would assign reading and then tell us everything that was in it. My plan did not yield guaranteed success. With the few assignments I turned in, and the high test scores I achieved, I just barely squeaked through high school. To this day, I have nightmares about not graduating because I never went to one of my classes during my senior year. After the first two weeks, I forgot it even existed! I made up for the poor grades by learning many life lessons in my adventures. (At least that's what I like to tell myself.)

The group of friends that I'd made through the plays consisted of mostly juniors and seniors. We often would get together for little parties. This group was a great influence on me. No drinking, smoking, or drugs. We played party games, went on picnics and had a lot of fun together. On St. Patrick's Day, the guys made green pancakes and other breakfast items for Loraine and me in a dressing room before an early performance of a play we were doing that day. It was amazing, exciting, and fun. And then a friend named Dave, a junior, asked me to his prom. One of our other friends asked Loraine. We were *so* excited! Freshmen going to the prom! We shopped for just the perfect dresses and planned everything from hair to shoes and nail polish. The plan was for the guys to pick us up at my house. We would go to dinner and the prom and then take part in an after-party at Dave's house. There were at least 20 of us, and we had so much fun. I don't think anyone fell asleep until morning.

With two schools come two proms. One of our other friends, Kristen, had asked Dave to go to our school's prom with her. It was ironic, because she and I had both bought and worn the same dress in the same color! Kristen and Dave hit it off, and they dated for a long time. I really didn't mind, because there were no real sparks between Dave and me.

I was an "odd duck" in the high school world. I got along with the popular crowd, the jocks, and the "drama geeks." Towards the end of my freshman year, I decided to have a party. I thought it would be a blast to invite people from all of the different crowds. I cleared it with my parents and began inviting people. What a blast! How often to you get the valedictorian, the "drama geeks," and the captains of every sports team at one party? At one point during the party, my brother called me to the door. A large group of guys were outside wanting to come in. I didn't know them and could tell the kind of party they had in mind wasn't my kind of party. I had made it clear to everyone I'd invited that there would be no alcohol. I didn't know the guys, and I turned them away. Sadly, I suspected Donny was with that crowd. I'd really lost my connection with him in high school, as he had turned to alcohol and drugs. I hated that there wasn't a damned thing I could do about it. I didn't know anything firsthand; it was only what I'd heard.

I went back downstairs to the party and resumed having a great time. The party was a great success. When things started to calm down, my immediate group of friends (the drama crowd) and I decided to go bowling. Not only did we have fun, my mom and brother cleaned up the basement bar area for me while we were gone. I was so thankful. Being the teen I was, I'm almost certain I didn't express my thanks as much as I should have.

chapter 7

Cracks in My Armor

It was either my sophomore or junior year when Dave's older brother, John, asked me to a movie. I was thrilled. Even though John was a year older than Dave, he was fun and kind. We had a good time and I had hoped that he would ask me out again. This was about the time my world came crashing down. One day I was sitting backstage with two of my closest friends, Stacie and Loraine. A guy I had dated during a recent play dumped me shortly after prom. I wasn't heartbroken, as he was an arrogant ass. Stacie told me that this guy had broken up with me so he could date her, and they were now a couple. This blow was immediately followed something more shocking: Loraine told me that John told her he had only asked me out because she already had a boyfriend. She was essentially done with said boyfriend and would be dating John. I snapped at that point. I started crying, and I couldn't stop. After crying for almost an hour, I went to my religion teacher's classroom for help.

I picked that particular teacher because she had noticed a comment on suicide in one of my papers. She wrote that if I ever felt that way, I needed to come to an adult right away. So I did. She took me to the vice principal's office. I respected Mr. O'Conner and had a great relationship with him. He talked to me for a while and then called my parents. It was agreed that I would start therapy immediately. The truth is, I wasn't crying over lost boyfriends. I was crying over the betrayal of two of my closest friends! How could not just one, but two of my best friends, do that to me?

Loraine and John ended up dating for well over a year. I also believe that he was the man to whom she lost her virginity. She always wanted to talk about John and how great things were and how much she loved him… *blah blah blah*. I just couldn't listen to it anymore. I pulled away from both Loraine and our group of friends.

The previous summer at the National Show-Skiing Tournament, I had been mesmerized by a video running in one of the booths featuring the best swivel skier I'd ever seen! The booth was for a ski school run by Water Ski Shows Inc. in Hollywood, Florida. I don't remember what the school cost, but I signed up immediately. I would be going over spring break. When I got home, I assured my parents that I would save up the money to pay for it myself. I always had a job, but I wasn't exactly making big money or good at saving it. I never did save enough, but I went to the school anyway. My parents paid for the school, and my brother Ryan, a sports writer who often traveled for work, gave me frequent flyer miles for the flight. (This was, and remained, a pattern in my life. I had a tendency to overcommit, and my family would always bail me out.) A senior who had interviewed me for an article in the school paper was really interested in joining the water-ski show team, and she decided to come with me to the school. After hearing his news, my parents felt much better about me going. They really shouldn't have, but I'll save that for later.

When spring break came, I headed down to Florida with my new friend, Penny. The ski school was *nothing* like I'd expected. Nobody met us at the airport when we arrived. Apparently there was some confusion about our flight time. In fact, the guy who was sent to pick us up didn't even know our full names or where we were from. He arrived by jeep and took us to the house where we would be staying during our week of training.

Situated on a small lake, the ranch house had three bedrooms, a master bedroom, and two additional rooms with two sets of bunk beds each. An additional set of bunk beds also was in the living room. (I use the term "bunk bed" loosely. These were homemade with thin mattresses. The bottom bunk was on the floor.) There was no food in the house, and when you wanted to get food it was like moving a mountain to get someone to take you to get groceries. (Because I already had a weight complex, I didn't push too hard. I decided that if nobody else seemed to need food, neither did I.)

Early every morning we were taken to the ski site at Sea World in Hollywood, Florida, and escorted out to a floating dock where we would stay until lunch. We took turns skiing. That week, the only students were me, Penny, and two other girls who seemed to know everyone already. I felt very isolated; once again, I was the youngest person there and was often ignored, except when I skied. The instructors were very impressed with both my swivel and trick skiing. They were also impressed that I could jump, but I didn't feel compelled to demonstrate. A wonderful man who was both a skier and a stunt man worked with me every day on the trampoline to teach me a back flip on a trick ski. I really wanted to learn that! I loved the trampoline, and it got me off of that floating dock for some quiet time. As for my swivel skiing, they really couldn't offer me much. It turned out that the female instructor on duty that week was no better than I was. Instead, they tried to teach me to swivel on my right foot rather than my left. In the U.S., all professional shows had right-foot-forward swivel lines. I could ski on my right foot, but I found it difficult to swivel on it. (It is like trying to write your name with your non-dominant hand; you can do it, but it's not always pretty.) They also mentioned a show in Australia that used left-foot-forward female skiers, and I was a good enough swivel skier that they offered me a job. I tried to explain that I was still in high school and couldn't just pack up and move to Australia. I kept that offer in mind, and intended to take it when I graduated from high school. Unfortunately, by that time, the Australia show had closed down.

I was determined to learn two new tricks that week. One was a new start for my swivel act. It was called a "sliding-toe start." I stood on the dock with my left foot in my swivel ski, and my right foot in a toehold in the rope. In theory, the boat would pull me sliding off of the dock and I would have my hands free and immediately be able to turn backwards while doing ballet moves with both arms. I had seen it done at the National Show Skiing tournament the previous summer. If that skier could do it, so could I! I'm pretty sure everyone thought I was nuts. We first tried it using a jumper instead of my swivel ski, and that was easy enough. Then we tried it with guys holding my hands as I slid off of the dock. I just couldn't master it on a swivel ski without a way to lock down the binding. Eventually, I remembered that the woman who had done it at Nationals had used a ballet move to reach down and unlock her binding after the start. My ski was older and didn't have a locking option. It was 360 degrees or nothing. I had also seen a trick called a 720 overhead. Just as the name sounds, the rope was pulled over your head while you spun 720 degrees. I'd been doing 360 overheads for years now. How much harder could it be to turn once more around? The answer was a lot! The amount of torque when I came around that second time always pulled me straight forward with the front of my thighs smacking the front of the ski. They were black and blue for a very long time.

When the ski day was over, we were taken back to the house where we either ordered pizza or were lucky enough to have someone drive us to a restaurant. Guys were coming in and out all the time. I was thrilled to be noticed by a guy named Scott. He was 21, and I don't think he realized I was 15. One night, everyone else had gone to their rooms and he and I were alone in the living room. He started kissing me and things heated up much faster than I was prepared for. There was some touching and then petting and I was terrified. I realized that I had gone along the whole time, but I needed to stop. Thankfully, about that time one of the other guys came in and interrupted us. I used that as my excuse to retreat to my room.

I thought that Penny would be my friend and confidant all week. I couldn't have been more wrong. Instead, she flirted with everyone and dismissed me as a child. She acted the same way after joining the ski team. I don't know if there was a guy on the team she didn't sleep with. That went for many of the women on the team. These were my role models? Spring break ended and we returned to school.

chapter 8

Starting Again

As I entered my junior year, I made up my mind that I wanted to date the man who was the captain of both the basketball and soccer teams. I didn't know anything about him other than he was cute, a senior, and well known. At the "back-to-school" dance, I put on an air of cocky confidence that I didn't really feel. I walked up to him and said, "Do you want to dance, Tim?" He looked down his nose at me for a minute. This only served to piss me off. I said, "Don't give me that look! You're no better than the rest of us." He led me by the hand to the dance floor and kissed me by the end of the first song. We went out with some people we both knew after the dance and made out all night. When I got home, I was floating on air—even more so the next day when he called and asked me to a movie. I was running around the house saying, "I'm going out with Tim Sobcheck!" After that first date, we were inseparable. I made it clear to him that I was still a virgin and intended to keep it that way. I also made it clear that I wanted nothing to do with someone who did drugs. The fact that I said that out loud should have been a sign that my intuition was telling me something.

As we prepared for a performance of *The Sound of Music*, I became friends with a girl named Jane. We had hung out and gone to some events together. Both of our boyfriends were now on the soccer team, so we went to all of the games together. I knew Jane came from money, but nothing could have prepared me for the first time I went to her house! I may have been too young to drive or a car wasn't available, so my Dad drove me to

Jane's house. As we arrived down a circle drive, my dad and I both had to lift our jaws off of the floor. It was the biggest house I'd ever visited! The façade featured a huge double door. I rang the bell, and when Jane answered the door I was standing there laughing so hard I could barely stand up. I said *"Really? This is where you live?"* She didn't seem fazed. She led me into the foyer. It was too much to take in at once. The interior included marble floors and a spiral staircase. To my right was a large formal dining room that could seat twenty people comfortably. On my left was a large formal living room that I didn't think anyone ever used. Past the living room was a split level with a family room above and a game room below. Directly in front of me, a sliding glass door led to an incredible indoor pool! Both the family room and game room had floor-to-ceiling windows overlooking the pool.

My junior year of high school was so much fun! Tim and I were on the homecoming court. I watched him play every basketball and soccer game, and I became friends with the girlfriends of the other jocks. I laughed off a number of party invitations from people who didn't even talk to me before I was with Tim. He was kind and gentle when we were alone. We spent most of our time in the living room above his parent's bar, cuddling and driving each other to complete sexual frustration. I had always gone to Catholic school and had been taught that my virginity was something to be cherished and that I should save it for marriage. Tim often tried to get me to "go all the way," but he always understood and backed down when I wouldn't. By now, I knew that I was the only one in my group of friends who was still a virgin. I also knew it was unlikely that I'd wait until marriage—but I still had to wait until I *knew* that it was right for me. When we were around his friends, Tim could be a real ass, barking out orders to me, like "get me a soda." It would usually backfire, as I would reply, "Go get your own damned soda!" On the rare occasion when the basketball team lost a game, I would get him the soda. They won the state title that year, but by then I was no longer Tim's girlfriend. I guess he got tired of waiting for me to "give it up" and found someone who would. I was crushed, but I tried not to show it too much. Actually, I never really knew him that well. He showed me exactly what he thought I wanted him to be and I saw exactly what I'd wanted to see. Looking back, I remembered a party at his house where the door to the living room was closed. I walked in and a couple of guys rushed to hide what they were doing. Since Tim wasn't in there, I let it go. Three or four years later, I learned through a mutual friend that Tim had been dealing drugs during the entire time we had been dating. I was stunned, and at first I didn't believe it. But this friend had known Tim well and I realized then that a number of things had never quite added up. He never worked but always seemed to have plenty of money. I had remained blissfully ignorant.

Jane became my best friend and we did everything together that year. I often slept over at her house and began to learn that a big house wasn't always a great thing. If we were in the family room and I needed something from the bedroom, it was a long walk. The kitchen in her house was the size of the entire first floor in my house. She had her own car and drove us everywhere. One Halloween weekend when her parents were out of town, she drove us around in her dad's DeLorean. (This was at the height of the *Back to the Future* era.) We were noticed everywhere we went! We drove through a parking lot where there was a haunted house and a radio broadcast booth. The broadcasters started yelling, "Hey, girls in the DeLorean! If you stop and come through the haunted house, we'll let you go for free." And so we stopped. It felt so amazing and unreal! Sadly, Jane was a year older than I was. After two great years of friendship, she moved on to college.

PART 2

Love Hurts

"When one is in love, one always begins by deceiving one's self, and one always ends by deceiving others. That is what the world calls a romance." ~ **Oscar Wilde**

chapter 9

I'll Never Be Me Again

The summer between my junior and senior year would change the course of my life forever. One of the women from the ski team asked me to come to a campground and stay with her and her children before the National Show Ski Tournament. We went up a few days early and, by Friday, I was getting restless. Once she and her kids were in bed, I was bored. It was July 29, 1988, and a dance was taking place at the campground. I walked over to look for someone my own age. I watched everyone dance and soon had my eye on a guy who was *very* good looking. When he went around to the back of a building where the bathrooms were located, I perched myself on a fence alongside the building so he had to walk right past me when he returned. He didn't walk past. He stopped and he flirted and we talked. We danced a couple of songs and, before I knew it, he asked if I wanted to go for a walk. Of course I did. We held hands and talked as we walked through the campground. It was such a beautiful walk through a beautiful campground with a beautiful man. I never realized where he was leading me. He took me towards his campsite to meet his friends. But I don't even remember any friends.

Only after we started kissing did I realize that he'd taken me far enough from the other campers so nobody could hear my screams. When I tried to stop him, there was no stopping. I kept saying "No! No! No! Please stop!" He put his hand over my mouth and told me to be quiet or someone would hear me. I begged and cried and begged some more. I kept thinking that if only I could just convey to him that I was a virgin and wanted to stay that way, then he would let go. He didn't. At one point, he pushed me to my knees and told me that if I wouldn't let him "fuck" me, then I'd better "get him off" this way. As he rammed his penis into my mouth, I bit him as much out of shock as out of fear and rage. That didn't go over well. I had been the last virgin in my group of friends. I had dated "the man on campus" and still kept my virginity. That night, I had it taken from me by a man who had me pinned down as I screamed for him to stop.

I honestly cannot tell you how I walked away from there or what was said. Somehow, I made it back to my tent in some kind of trance. I went to change my clothes and saw the blood in my panties that had spread to my white pants. I was so ashamed. How could I have been so stupid? How could I have gone for a walk with a perfect stranger? How could I have let him do that to me? I couldn't even grasp the fact that I'd been raped. I thought it was my own fault for leading him on. I remembered the eagle tattoo on one of his arms. The next day, I saw that tattoo at the pool by the lodge as we were leaving and was struck with terror. I searched for someone or something to hide behind. We left the campsite and went on to the National Show Ski Tournament as if everything was normal. For me, there would be no such thing as normal ever again. I now knew what men were really like, what they really wanted, and that everything else was just a ploy to get you to the end game. I would never be anybody's victim like that again.

I didn't tell anyone about this for several days. It haunted my every waking moment and was tearing me apart. Finally, the dam broke the following Tuesday. I told my best friend on the ski team, Michelle. She was only 15, two years younger than me, but she was very mature and a great friend. She received a lot of attention from everyone on the team from the moment she joined. I would have liked to hate her for that, but she was kind and fun. She immediately said, "I can't handle this myself. I need to tell Shane." He was a good friend of hers, a twenty-something guy on the team. We had been cleaning a laundry mat for one of the ski team members when I told her. Within a few minutes after Michelle's call, Shane pulled up in his little red sports car. I left the building because I just couldn't listen. I stood outside by my car crying. Minutes later, Shane had me wrapped in his strong arms. He told me to be ready the following day at noon, because he was coming by to pick me up. He took me to a hospital where I was examined. Then he took me to a counselor and sat there and held my hand as I told the counselor what had happened. (At least the parts I wasn't most ashamed of.) The counselor was required by law to report the incident to the police. Shane convinced me that I needed to tell my parents before the police did. He not only drove me home, but came in with me and held my hand as I told my mother. I couldn't even look her in the eye, but Shane held my hand tightly and encouraged me to go on. I wasn't around when my mom told my dad and brothers, but I remember walking past the room and seeing them all with their heads in their hands; it looked like they were crying.

Shane and I would go back to our usual roles in the ski team, and no one ever knew how much he had supported me. I will never forget Shane's act of kindness during that horrific time. He literally saved my life.

I was so ashamed about what happened. Despite all the people and counselors telling me it wasn't my fault, I thought, "If they only knew the whole truth, they would know it *was* my fault." My family sent me for counseling, but I told them I wanted to stop going and that I was fine. My mom tried a few times to get me to talk about it with her, but I never would. I couldn't even open up to a counselor, because I was too ashamed of my behavior. I had intentionally worn flattering clothes, made him notice me, and then went for a walk to the middle of nowhere where I was a willing participant in the kissing that followed. I should have known that the expectation was sex! I would carry that guilt within me for the next twenty years.

Even though I have worked through my guilt and shame over this incident, I felt my barrier walls go up again just by writing about what had happened. Those walls protected my heart for twenty years, but they did irrevocable damage to my body, my spirit, my soul, and my ability to feel emotion.

chapter 10

Life After

When my senior year started, I went out one night with my original gang of friends before they all had to be back at college. We went moonlight bowling. At one point, I walked up to the counter for something and I could sense that the guy who worked there was stressed out. He also was cute. I commented on his stress and he said, "You want a job?" I thought about it for a minute and said "Sure. Give me an application." I filled it out right there and was called back within days.

The manager called me in for an interview and handed me a new application. He admitted that the guy I met working the counter, Roger, had begged him to hire me, but my application was too sloppy and incomplete because I had filled it out while I was busy bowling. He made me fill it out again and then hired me on the spot. I knew I'd been hired for my looks, but I didn't care. I thought this was the best job in the world for a high school girl! I began working the counter, trained by a girl named Samantha, aka "Sam." She went on and on about Roger being *so* happy they hired me and what a nice guy he was and how he really wanted to date me. The day finally came when Roger was training me. We got to know each other a bit, and he asked me out shortly thereafter. He had already graduated, so it was a bit difficult to navigate our relationship when I still wanted to do social things at school. He refused to go to the winter dance with me, so I didn't go. But he made it up to me by taking me out for a nice dinner. When my senior prom finally came around, he agreed to go. At the time, I felt like Cinderella. I'd bought a very expensive dress that was just so "perfect." When I look back at those pictures, all I can think is, "What the hell was I thinking?" I had burgundy hair in a long fluffy mullet, and it completely clashed with my pink metallic dress. Ouch! The '80s were not good for fashion. Roger was a good sport—considering that we sat with all of my girlfriends, and one of them brought her girlfriend as a date. That wasn't exactly the rage in 1989.

I loved my job at the bowling alley. I usually worked leagues during the week and then moonlight bowling on Friday and Saturday nights. I also started to realize that I wasn't ugly or invisible. Numerous guys hit on me regularly, and that did *wonders* for my self-esteem. Roger was wonderful to me. He would leave roses and cards in my car on a regular basis. After about nine months of dating, we finally had my first experience with consensual sex—on *my* terms. Roger was kind and gentle. He knew that my only experience with intercourse had been the rape. Up to this point, Roger and I had pretty much done "everything but." My first consensual sex wasn't nearly as special as I'd imagined it would be. We were at his house and nobody was home, but I had a constant fear that someone would come home! We were in his waterbed, which made things difficult. I wasn't even sure we did it right. As my high school days came to an end, so did my relationship with Roger. He was sweet but also kind of boring. I didn't want to be put on a pedestal. I wanted someone who would challenge me when I was wrong. I knew that I'd be going away right after my high school graduation and would be gone for the next year. I wanted to be free to explore and date, not tied down to someone I'd never see.

Earlier in my senior year, I saw an ad in *Water Ski Magazine* looking for waterski instructors for summer camps. That sounded a *lot* more fun than "going pro." Female professional show skiers are required to step on a scale daily. When their weight exceeds 120 pounds, they're benched. I was in great shape, but 120 would never be realistic for me. I was solid muscle. So, I responded to the magazine ad with a cover letter, résumé, and photo. It didn't take long for my contract to arrive by mail. All I had to do was sign it and I would have a job for the summer in Waterville, Maine. The salary wouldn't cover my airfare, but it was worth the adventure! Once again, my brother Ryan came through with frequent flyer miles. Once I was there, I wouldn't have many expenses. All room and board at camp was covered.

After breaking up with Roger and before leaving for Maine, I went on what I now call a "Trampage." Oprah Winfrey once said something like, "Nobody wakes up one morning and says to herself, 'I'm going to be extremely promiscuous from now on.'" Rape victims who don't follow through with counseling go in one of two directions: they're either afraid to be touched at all, or they have *a lot* of sex. I fell into the second category.

So many twisted beliefs and justifications swam around in my head at the time. One was, "If I don't say 'no,' he can't rape me." This was the case with the first man I dated after Roger. He also worked at the bowling alley and had been actively pursuing me for some time. We went out a few times. One day, when we were alone at my parent's house, things got out of hand. Instead of saying "no," I went right along as if it had been my intention all along. That allowed me to feel like I'd had some say or control, which I didn't. I had sex simply because I was afraid to say "no." I had seen the result of that and didn't care to relive it. In hindsight, I relived it many times over for the simple reason that I was afraid to say "*No!*" Not that there wouldn't be plenty of times in the future when I was the aggressor with something to prove, but there were just as many times when I went along with sex for fear of reliving that horrific experience of being held down and simply having it taken from me.

Once I was no longer a virgin, I also wanted to prove what a woman I was to men who had dismissed me in the past because I was too young or wasn't willing to sleep with them. The next man I slept with fell into this category. He and I had "been together" at the previous waterski convention, but I would not have sex with him. Once that summer, I watched him flirt with one of the other girls (known to be a complete tramp) standing right next to me. He barely glanced in my direction; I wasn't even sure if he recognized me. For some reason, he felt like "unfinished business," as if I somehow needed to *make* him remember me. I took two of my girlfriends with me one night to see his performance at a waterski show. We went back to his house after the show. I felt kind of sleazy after we had sex in his bed, with my girlfriends in the other room, so I got up and got dressed.

I didn't leave my number or even ask for his. I just left while he lay there in bed. My girlfriends told me later that I was wearing my shirt inside out. I couldn't help but wonder what I'd been thinking. *That* certainly did not feel like any kind of victory.

chapter 11

Spreading My Wings

efore long, it was time to fly to Maine to teach waterskiing at a
children's summer camp. I was thrust into a world that was completely
foreign to me, both literally and figuratively. Upon arrival at the Portland
airport (which has to be the smallest airport ever!), something happened
that has remained with me like it just happened yesterday. I was sitting in
a chair with my bags, nervously waiting for the bus that would pick up me
and the other counselors and take us to the camp. I watched the escalator,
and a guy about my age was coming up. He wore a blue-and-white-striped,
button-down shirt with a saxophone case hanging from his neck. He had
bushy hair, but he was cute! I wondered if he was a camp counselor, too. In
my youthful naiveté, I sensed that we were meant to be "lovers"—but we
didn't even meet then. We met on the bus that took us to camp. His name
was Noah, and he was from Florida. He had just graduated from high
school, as I had, and was planning to go to school just north of Chicago
at Northwestern University the following fall. I would be in Minneapolis
attending a trade school in travel agency operations.

I chose a trade school, because I didn't think I could get into college.
I had convinced myself that I would be done with school and would have
a career for years before my friends graduated. My grades were poor, and I
took that to mean I wasn't smart. Actually, I was as smart as anyone; others
just happened to turn in their homework once in a while. I was always in
a hurry to grow up. Throughout my life, I had been defined as being the
"youngest." I was always the youngest person in every situation. Now that

I was old enough so I couldn't be the youngest, I had to find other ways to prove myself.

Counselor orientation took place during the first week of camp. We slowly started getting to know each other. Half of the counselors were from Europe. When we blended together, it was as if we'd created our own country. Noah and I hung out a bit that first week. I discovered he was going to be a waterski instructor like me. The third waterski instructor, Jay, had been to the camp the summer before. As Noah and I walked around the grounds one night, we began kissing. I'm pretty sure I initiated it. Just as things were heating up, Noah told me he had a girlfriend back home and he wanted to be faithful to her. Wow! I did not see that coming! We went our separate ways that night, with what I thought were no hard feelings.

Once the kids arrived, it got pretty crazy pretty fast! I spent almost every moment of every day in a boat or in the water helping kids learn to ski. Noah was going to be a music major, and I had been a singer in high school, so whenever we were working in the same boat, we would harmonize songs all day. It was fun. Some kids were easier to teach than others. Both Jay and Noah had been recreational skiers, so they weren't prepared for the techniques I used to help those who were not so easily taught. If the children were really little, I'd often take them up in my arms and then set them down on my own skis, just as my brothers had done with me many years earlier. For the slightly more ready, I would put them on their own skis, between my skis, and put my arms under theirs on the rope. Once we were up, I would let go and they would be off and skiing solo. As summer flew by at a frenzied pace, I was enjoying every minute of it. I had a cabin with some of the youngest kids in camp and a couple of great fellow counselors, one of whom had become my best friend at camp, a swimming instructor named Audrey.

On the 4th of July, we took the kids on a field trip to see the fireworks. That night I happened to sit next to a Welsh rugby player named Tate. The sky wasn't the only place fireworks were going off. Audrey had warned me about Tate. Apparently they had both been at camp the summer before and Tate had earned himself a reputation for being somewhat of a bad boy. I might as well have just walked over to his cabin the moment she warned me about him. If there was a bad boy around, I was bound to fall for him.

This night was no different. (Actually, it was hard to see him as a "bad boy" when he carried his rugby ball with him everywhere *and* sucked his thumb.) I thought he was adorable. We spent more time looking into one another's eyes than we did watching the children—or the fireworks. By the time we got back to the bus, a few of the more observant kids were already chanting, "Bridgette and Tate, sitting in a tree…." This just happened to be a night when we were both without camp responsibilities after "lights out" for the kids. We met and walked around the grounds, holding hands and getting to know each other. On the second night we were together, he led me to the open gym and we had sex right there on the mats. When we finished, he said, "I didn't think you'd let me do that." I replied, "Neither did I." From then on, we spent every moment together that we could. It wasn't easy. We were up as early as 6:00 a.m. most days and stayed out together until 2:00 a.m. We even worked it out so that I would no longer have to pull skiers during the morning "free period." Tate was the rifle instructor. The rifle range was the one place in camp where nobody could enter without calling down for permission. Every day during the morning free period, I snuck off to the rifle range where we would make love, with whatever time we had. In my heart, we were making love and not just having sex. I had fallen—and fallen hard!

Tate taught me about sex. He taught me to truly enjoy it and to ask for what I wanted and to learn what he wanted. He empowered me in a way I had never been before. I learned how to drive him insane, and he did the same for me. The only downside was that he wanted it *all the time!* We would be together every chance we got. On the dock. In the boats. On the soccer field. In the gym. In the stables. If we could find a place at night that wasn't occupied, we were there making love.

It was common for counselors with a day off to leave camp the night before and stay in a hotel. Tate and I hung out with three close friends: Jay, the third water-ski instructor; Audrey; and a swim instructor named Ron. One night, the five of us shared a hotel room. Tate and I slept in one bed, while Jay, Audrey, and Ron shared the other. When Tate thought everyone else was asleep, he kept trying to get me to have sex with him. No matter how many times I said "no," he knew it was just a matter of time before I would give in. He knew all of my "secret places." Eventually, he was on top of me, and I was trying to be really quiet! Audrey—you had to love her—sat up and yelled, "Ahhhhh, they're *shunting!*" (This is British slang for having sex.) Of course, by then everyone was awake and I was mortified.

I would have killed Tate if I weren't so completely head over heels for him.

Life carried on like that until one day, late in the summer, when a bunch of us had a day off. We had rented a hotel room and been drinking for a good long time. Noah was *not* a good drunk! For some reason, he decided it was a good idea to tell everyone, including Tate, that he and I had made out before I was with Tate. I was humiliated! Good Lord! I thought everyone thought of me as a slut. I left the room crying to cool off outside. Tate came out and said he wasn't bothered by it at all. I didn't think I could ever forgive Noah for embarrassing me like that. We didn't talk much for the rest of that summer. I didn't expect to ever hear from him again.

As the summer wound down, I dreaded the moment when I had to say goodbye to Tate. I'll never forget the last night we had together. All of the kids had left camp by then. The counselors all went out to a bar, but it was one with an age restriction that prevented me from joining them. (Normally I had opposite nights off with a British girl who looked a lot like me, and she would let me use her passport. I could do a great British accent by then.) I resented the fact that Tate had gone in the bar without me, but there was nothing I could do. I joined one of the other female counselors, who also was underage, and we walked across a parking lot to a store. I bought my first piece of lingerie. It was a white teddy with lots of lace. The gang left the bar early and we all went to a convenience store about a mile from camp. We sat on picnic tables and drank beer. Tate and I decided to walk back to camp alone. I was angry because it was our last night together; it didn't seem to matter to him at all. I expressed my feelings, only to be shocked when he dropped to his knees, crying, and clinging to my legs! That was as close to an "I Love You" as I ever expected to get from Tate. We went back to my cabin, which had been vacated by my roommates for the night. I went into the bathroom and changed into my new teddy and watched his jaw drop as I walked out.

We made love over and over again and held each other all night. He planned to stay in the States for a while after camp, so we agreed he would come to Milwaukee two days after I returned. At least this goodbye wasn't final.

The flight home felt long and lonely. When I walked off of the plane, my whole family *and* Roger were standing at the gate waiting for me! It felt great to be home, but I missed Tate every minute we were apart. My family arranged a big dinner in honor of my coming home, and my mother invited Roger to join us. While we were sitting in the living room a bit later, one of my brothers said, "So when's this guy from England supposed to get here?" I stumbled. I glanced at Roger and answered my brother with a quick, "In two days." He was slow to realize that I hadn't told Roger about Tate. Roger and I went outside and I said, "There's something I need to tell you." He responded, "You met a guy at camp named Tate, he's from England (by now I'd given up on correcting everyone that Tate actually was from Wales), and he'll be here in two days." When I confirmed all of this, Roger said, "I don't understand. You said you didn't want a long-distance relationship, and then you come home with a boyfriend from *England!*" I did what I could to explain, but I was sure he never understood.

Two days later, I picked Tate up at the airport. It was *so* wonderful! I couldn't wait to be in his arms again! He was staying on the sleeper sofa upstairs in the room right next to mine; of course, neither of us slept alone! I showed Tate around Milwaukee, including the art museum. (I wouldn't have pegged him for the art museum type!) I took him to the bowling alley where I worked and we sat around and drank with my friends. They all started calling him "Mate" and loved his accent. Sadly, our time together eventually had to end. I took him to the airport, kissed him goodbye, and bawled my eyes out. I was so depressed that nothing consoled me. Mom tried. She even offered me money to go shopping, but I didn't want to move. I just lay on the couch and cried. I was sure I had found my soulmate, but unfortunately we lived on opposite sides of the world.

chapter 12

Life Goes On

I had a few months before I had to leave for school, so I filled shifts at the bowling alley to earn some money. I began filling in as a cocktail waitress, and discovered I could make a lot more money as a waitress than on the counter. The tips were great. I continued flirting with every shift. When the Professional Bowling Association tour came to town, I met a man with whom I clicked. His name was Pat. I didn't do more than kiss him while he was in town, but we did keep in touch. Those were the days before cell phones and email, so it was an occasional letter or phone call.

Fall came, and I left Milwaukee and headed to school in Minneapolis. I was staying in an all-girls dorm that was *very* strict. My first roommate was named Heather. I thought we got along just fine, but she was much less social than I was. I had made a lot of friends in the dorms, and we would go out on weekends or stay in the dorms and drink.

We must have made quite a sight as we waited to catch a bus on Hennepin Avenue (which I later learned was where most of the city's prostitutes did their business). We were a group of about 10 girls, all of 18 years old and dressed like little tramps. Most of the girls were beautiful, stick-thin blondes, and I often felt invisible when we went out together. A number of times we went to a club on the University of Minnesota campus called The Underground. The bar allowed anyone over 18 into the club, but you would only get a wristband to buy drinks if you were over 21. It was easy to get guys to buy us drinks. I'll never forget one night when I was drinking my beer and a guy came up and asked to see my wristband. I replied, "Yeah, sure." He said, "No seriously, I'm club security." I said, "Yeah, right" as I downed the rest of my beer. He wasn't kidding. He was club security and I was out the door. That was the night when I did one of the most dangerous things ever in my life: I allowed a strange man talk me into letting him drive me to his home. By the time I looked at my watch, it was after 1:00 a.m. and the dorm doors were locked. If you rang the bell to wake the staff, you were given some sort of penalty. Somehow, going home with a total stranger was far less scary than waking up the staff. I was drunk and stupid. I told him numerous times that I was accompanying him *just to sleep*. He agreed. He let me go to sleep when got to his place, but we slept in the same bed. I awoke to his fingers and mouth working slow magic on me. We had sex that morning, and then he drove me to the dorms. It's bothered me through the years that I never remembered his name. I didn't ask for his number and he didn't ask for mine. It might as well have been a transaction. The only thing missing was the cash.

By then, I had made friends with some more "normal" girls on my floor, including my roommate Heather and a girl named Jody who lived at the end of the hall. They had guy friends who lived in the area. Thanks to my summer camp experience, I could now do a *perfect* English accent. It was our version of "stupid party tricks." One day, as I walked down the hall, I heard Jody say into the phone; "We have an exchange student here from England. Do you want to talk to her? (For anyone under 25—there was a time when all phones plugged into a wall. In the dorms, the only phones were in a central hallway.) I took the phone and held a brief conversation with one of her friends. From that moment on, I wasn't just plain old Bridgette. I was the exotic exchange student that all of Jody's friends wanted to meet. It was so insane! They even arranged to have a party at their apartment just so they could meet me. The guys picked us up at the dorms. I spent about the first three hours speaking in a perfect English accent, without slipping even once. Finally, I'd grown tired of this charade. I said (still in my accent), "Boys, I've got to tell you something." When they asked what, I dropped the accent and said, "I'm from Milwaukee." I had to spend the next two hours convincing them I wasn't really from England. It was so absurd it was funny. One of the guys in that group, Bryan, was very interested in me. Jody was already dating his friend Wayne, so connecting with Bryan would have been very convenient. Bryan was sweet, but I still hoped things would work out with Tate the following summer. I was honest with Bryan about the fact that I wasn't really looking for a relationship. At some point, while walking the grounds of the apartment complex, we ended up having sex in the sauna. (*Note:* In this book I often say "having sex" or "had sex." That is in the context of the grown-up me. Back then, I was still naïve enough to think of it as "making love.") We dated briefly, and then one night I saw the true colors of both Bryan and Wayne. I don't remember what couple started fighting first, but both Jody and I ended up hiding in a neighboring apartment until the guys calmed down. One thing I did *not* want in a relationship was that kind of drama. I think that was the last time I saw Bryan.

One day I received a call from Pat, the bowler from the PBA tour. He wanted to come and spend the weekend with me in Minneapolis. I was so excited. I made hotel reservations at the hotel closest to the dorms. (*No* men were allowed in the dorms.) I bought a cute camisole in the lingerie section at a local department store. To be honest, making a list of things he wanted to do in Minneapolis was the last thing I thought we'd be doing. I figured we'd spend the entire weekend in bed, ordering room service. By the end of the first day of our time together, he was restless and wanted to get out of the room. It was the middle of winter and *very* cold outside. Luckily, we were just a couple of blocks from the entrance of the city's skyway system. I escorted him from building to building along the skyway, and we ended up at a mall. There really wasn't much else we could do. We didn't have a car and I didn't know the area once I was more than six blocks from my school in any direction. We went back to the hotel and spent the rest of his visit in bed. Once he returned to Vegas, I never heard from him again. I was very angry. I felt like I was "unfinished business" to him, and now that he had slept with me, we were done. I sent him a letter to that effect but never heard from him again. Looking back, it's clear that I was the one who appeared interested in just having sex—not him. It was my own fault. I assumed that was the only reason a man would fly in to see me. It couldn't have been my sparkling personality. My self-esteem was pretty low at that point.

No Really. You Can't Make This Stuff Up!

Quite a number of other events in the travel school dorms shaped my life. One day I came home to find that Heather had moved out without telling me. She had arranged to move in with Jody when *her* roommate moved out. I was assigned a new roommate named Annie, who didn't attend my school. She moved here from a few states away where she had been frequently abused and raped by family members. She was all alone in the world. That was hard for me to comprehend, as I didn't think I'd ever be so alone. As much as I tried to bond with Annie, it became harder and harder to do so. All she would ever talk about was her abuse and her issues. I was tired of being a 24/7 counselor. One day I came home from school and fell into bed for a nap. I thought I heard Annie come in, but when I got up, I didn't see her. I walked down the hall to hang with my friends, and after a while I started asking if anyone had seen her. Nobody had. I had a sinking feeling as I walked back to my room. I tried her closet door and it was locked from the inside. I started banging on it and she told me to go away. I told her I couldn't do that and that she needed to open the door. When she finally did, she was sitting on a box. One wrist was bloody and she was holding a razor blade in the other hand. I calmly and slowly convinced her to give me the blade, and when she did, I ran like hell to the dorm lady's room and pounded on the door. I was so upset I couldn't even speak. She kept saying, "What is it?" All I could say was, "Annie!!" She said, "Annie what?" I just made a slashing motion across my wrist. She called 911 and went to my room. I stayed away, relieved to be free of that responsibility. I wanted to let the adrenaline running through my body settle down. That's when one of the firefighter/EMTs walked out into the hall and asked, "Are you Bridgette?" When I said yes, he explained that Annie would not let them come near her. He asked if I would please come and talk to her. When I walked back into our room, Annie was standing on the bed like a caged animal and would not let anyone near her. I thought this was a little too dramatic, but I talked her down. She made me promise I would ride to the hospital with her in the ambulance. I didn't *want* to ride with her. She had just scared the shit out of me and I was mad as hell! But somehow I did what she asked. As soon as I got her settled in at the hospital, I caught the first cab back to the dorms. I was relieved when her belongings were moved out of my room shortly thereafter.

Another episode happened very late one night. I heard pounding and screaming at a friend's door at the end of the hall. I was pissed off and jumped out of bed. I was about to swing my door open and tell this person just what I thought of her morning antics when I realized she sounded completely crazy. I waited a few minutes and she was gone. A couple of seconds later, my friends were pounding on my door begging me to let them in so they could hide. I never really learned the whole story, but I know it had something to do with them deciding to smoke pot with this woman. (Genius, I know.) Something didn't go as planned or they did something; I'll never know. I didn't sleep that night and I was tired during classes the next day. I returned to the dorms and was sitting on a sofa in the lobby when the woman in question walked in. I mumbled under my breath, "*Fucking psycho!*" She heard me and walked over and stood in front of me and said, "What did you say?" I stood up and replied, "I said you're a fucking psycho." Another girl in the lobby jumped into the conversation and backed me up. Some yelling ensued before the woman was escorted out of the lobby.

A day or two later, someone ran to my room to tell me I couldn't go to the cafeteria or lobby because that same woman had enlisted some "skinheads" to kill the five of us—and I was on the top of the list. Aww Crap! *Really?* Now this situation was getting too stupid for even fiction! I tried to call the police to get those people out of our building. They advised me that officers were already responding to the dorms, but in the meantime it might be best if I left town for a week or so. I called Adam, a former member of my ski team, because we had become good friends. He was now living in Rochester, Minnesota, about two hours south of the Twin Cities. I told him what had happened and he said he'd be on his way to get me. I actually received a police escort out to his car when he arrived. It was nice to stay at Adam's quiet riverfront house for the week. The first night, he had another friend staying over and we did some target shooting with a rifle. My gun kept getting stuck on the fifth bullet in the clip. That night, I had powerful nightmares about that woman coming after me, but my gun kept getting stuck. Adam's friend shook me awake. I had always thought myself in love with Adam, but he was four or five years older than me. That wouldn't have mattered if we'd met as adults, but we met when I was 14 and he was 19. That week was a chance to "play house." I pretended that everything was fine and enjoyed the house and wooded yard while he was at work and then had dinner with him every night. The only thing was, at bedtime, I went to the couch while he went to bed. I kept wondering if he slept as little as I did that week.

The following week, I returned to school a bit skittish, but I was assured that the "threat" had been averted and we were all safe. The semester continued on as if it had never happened. I got frequent calls from home, regular calls from Roger (I could tell he was hoping we'd get back together after the semester was over), Sam, and a few surprises. Tim—the guy I'd dated during my junior year—began to call regularly, but I was not at all sure how I felt about that. We talked frequently, and he wanted to go out when we both returned home from school. Audrey called to tell me that Tate was returning to camp that summer. I called my parents and said, "I know I'm supposed to get a job when I get home, but could I just wait for one more summer?" They understood. The biggest surprise of all was that Noah also called me at school a number of times. By the end of the semester, I knew that Audrey, Tate, Noah and I were all going back to camp. I looked forward to it so much! Perhaps you can catch lightning in a bottle!

I returned home in mid-April and didn't have to leave for camp until June 21. I started an internship at a travel agency and picked up some shifts at the bowling alley again.

One day in May, when I had been asleep on the couch, I woke to hear my mother on the phone with one of my brothers. She tried to talk quietly and in code, but that only served to awaken me fully. She was asking my brother Rodney if he thought this was a good car and one that I would like! Like it? *I loved it!* The beautiful, burgundy Chevy Camaro Berlinetta was only a couple of years old, and I was *so* excited! This was shortly after my grandparents had died, and my parents allotted part of the inheritance to each of us kids. They paid for the car with my inheritance, and I still owed them a couple thousand dollars, but it was *so* worth it! The first thing I asked was if I could take it to Maine for the summer. When at camp, I'd learned there were two things guaranteed to ensure you have a great time: a car, and an ID. My parents would only agree to let me take the car if someone rode with me. We arranged for Audrey to fly from Colorado to Milwaukee and then make the drive with me. Now that that was set, all I could do was work and wait.

On Friday and Saturday nights, I usually worked the counter at the bowling alley with a man named Brandon. He had been working there since I was away at school and Sam kept telling me how cute Brandon was and how funny he was or that he just did this or that. When returned home from school and started working there again, Brandon told Sam, "That's her!" Brandon had told Sam about a girl who used to work at the bowling alley who was the woman of his dreams. He was *very* hard to resist. I didn't. We started dating. (My memory was that all we ever did was sleep together, but researching my journal informed me that we actually went on real dates!) Oh, the musings in the mind of an 18 year old. I was head over heels for him after less than a week. It took about that long for us to start sleeping together, too. Unfortunately, Brandon wasn't exactly what you would call reliable. On too many occasions, he said he'd call and I would stay home and wait by the phone without ever having it ring. According to my journal, we "officially" broke up on Thursday, May 3, 1990.

I still cared about Brandon, so I was easy prey whenever he decided to pull my strings. He was selfish and narcissistic. He and I would cross one another's path often in the coming year, but I tried to never let the hurt show. About a month after we'd stopped dating, I began to feel sick all of the time. It was all I could do to drag myself to work and finish a shift. Then, my period that month was more spotting than bleeding. I was worried. We'd used protection, but what if? One night, I walked into the bowling alley with Sam and she stopped to talk to Brandon at the counter. He saw me and immediately said, "What's wrong?" (I suppose the Sprite I was drinking might have given it away.) I kept dodging the question and said we'd talk about it another time. He said, "You think you're pregnant, don't you?" Geez! Was I *that* easy to read? We went out to the parking lot and sat in the car to talk. At first, he tried to bring up abortion. I told him that was not an option. If he didn't want a baby, I would either raise it alone or give it up for adoption. We agreed that I would go to Planned Parenthood in the morning and call him as soon as I got home. I did. When he answered the phone, I said "Brandon, I have the best news!" He said, "You're pregnant!" When I said no, that I wasn't, he actually sounded disappointed! He said, "Aw, next week was supposed to be my holiday." Father's Day.

Thank goodness I had just had the test, because the following night I worked at the counter at the bowling alley and was talking to Roger on the phone. I told him I wasn't feeling well. The next thing I remember was waking up in an ambulance on the way to the hospital. My parents had been called and met us there. Roger said I had stopped making sense and that a manager had just come behind my counter when I collapsed. Doctors in a hospital always ask if you could be pregnant. Well, in front of my parents, the answer would always be "no!" Later, when they were out of the room I told the nurse about my trip to Planned Parenthood the day before. They confirmed those results and said they thought that I had been feeling ill due to migraine headaches. Whew! What a relief. I had been afraid I wouldn't be able to go to Maine! (To be clear, if I had been pregnant, Maine wouldn't have even crossed my mind. But I was afraid that my collapse meant there was something else wrong with me that would keep me from going.) By now, it was only two weeks away. I was *so* excited.

chapter 14

Lightning in a Bottle

udrey flew in to Milwaukee before we planned to leave. We enjoyed a night with the family and tried to get some sleep. The following morning, with the car packed to its absolute limit, we set off for Maine. We talked and laughed throughout the entire trip. We stayed in a couple of dive hotels. One night we got off the freeway in Pennsylvania and ended up in a place called "Prince Spaghettiville." We hoped find a liquor store and a hotel, but our exit didn't look promising. When we finally found a liquor store, it had bars on the windows. I waited in the car while Audrey went in to buy what we wanted. When she came out, she said the clerk told her we were lucky to get there alive. We got back on the freeway and kept driving until we saw a decent hotel sign. Whew! Looking back, it should have been terrifying for two young women driving across the country with no idea about bad neighborhoods and no cell phones or GPS, but for us it was nothing but fun! Every morning, we stopped for breakfast and then hit the road.

As we crossed the Maine border, we did our own dance in the car. We had one stop to make before we continued on to Waterville—the Department of Motor Vehicles in Augusta. I needed to get a Maine ID card to show I was over 21. Before we left, my sister-in-law had given me her birth certificate, marriage license, and a number of other documents. I walked into the DMV trying *very* hard not to let them see me sweat. I told myself I was playing a role and did my very best to play it well. I explained that my purse had been stolen along with all of my important identification.

I needed to get an ID card. They processed all of my paperwork and then asked for my signature. Oh *crap!* I'd forgotten to practice her signature. I did my best, but it was clearly still my handwriting. The man questioned me, saying, "The signature on your marriage license was a lot more bubbly than it is now." I came back with, "I was a hell of a lot more bubbly when I got married. I'm not so bubbly now!" I did my best to look like a woman disillusioned by life. He said he couldn't approve it right away. It would have to go through his supervisors. He told me they would mail it to my Maine address when or if it was approved. I walked out of there terrified. I was waiting to be arrested at any moment.

We finally pulled into camp about two hours later. I had never been so happy to arrive anywhere in my life. We first stopped in at the office and the secretary was so happy to see us both. I loved her to death. She wrapped us each in a warm hug. I informed her of my sister-in-law's name and that, if any mail should arrive for her, it would be for me. She just laughed at me when I told her the story.

We were given our cabin assignments and then we proceeded to settle in. For the first four-week session, I would be in charge of the five youngest girls. Because they were the most work, we supervised them with two counselors and one junior counselor. But, of course, the campers wouldn't arrive for another week. After we both settled in to our separate cabins, Audrey and I went to park the car in the lot and grab a cigarette—or as we referred to them, "peanuts." (I had been a social smoker on and off throughout most of my junior high and high school years, but never smoked regularly. This was more of a bonding ritual between us.) At the moment, I tried, unsuccessfully, to hide the fact that I was unbelievably nervous about seeing Tate again. Noah arrived not long after we did and he had a truck! We were so set for summer. Our own transportation was the key to fun on days and nights off. It guaranteed that we didn't have to wait for someone else to let us tag along.

When Tate finally arrived, I couldn't wait to get him alone and hopefully pick up where we left off. Sadly, that wasn't what he had in mind. He kept his distance and, when I tried to talk to him, he made it clear that he was *not* looking for a relationship that summer—"at least not one that means anything." I was devastated! I didn't know it was possible to feel your heart break that many times and have it keep beating. At least I would still have Audrey and Noah to hang out with all summer.

We also met a number of new counselors who seemed like they were going to be a lot of fun. About a week after we got there, my ID came in the mail. I let my breath out for the first time since being at the DMV. I had secretly been waiting for the police to show up and arrest me at any time. I now had a car and an ID! I could go anywhere I wanted and do anything. I also was sure I'd never have to look for people with whom to hang out. They most certainly would be coming to me to ask what I was doing and could they come along.

By the time the kids arrived, Audrey had met and fallen for a new counselor from England named Joe. Noah had met and fallen for a new counselor from England named Sue. I had never felt so incredibly alone in my life. I was heartbroken over losing Tate, and my only two friends in the camp were spending every free minute with their new loves.

I was assigned to supervise a field trip to take a group of kids to an auction and buy some animals for our petting zoo. One of the animals we bought was a baby bunny that we eventually named BB, as in Bridgett's baby. Whenever I found myself with free time, I walked over to the petting zoo and cuddled the bunny. That bunny was my comfort in a world that had just shifted. Sadly, one day, one of the kids set the bunny down in the grass and he was gone, too. I cried over a bunny!

I had a few good times that summer. I was now the "Water Ski Director," so I made the assignments every day. The third water ski instructor that summer was a guy from Texas named Scott. He was kind and competent enough, but not always the sharpest knife in the drawer. After a week or two, we settled into the routine of Scott taking his own boat and me and Noah taking the other. We had fun while teaching. Once again, Noah and I sang songs all day—and even perfected a couple for camp events. Sue, Noah's new love from England, did *not* like me at all. She saw me as a threat for her guy's attention. We had to be sure she never found us alone together or she would go ballistic.

One day, only three of us were off work: me, Tate, and a new counselor named Kurt. We decided to go to Acadia National Park that day. On the way, we saw a miniature golf course and decided to stop and play. After we were back on the road, we saw a giant water slide and we stopped. Tate somehow talked them into letting us in for free. We played on that waterslide for hours and never did make it to the national park. It was the best kind of day, because we didn't stick to any itinerary or plan. We just rolled through the day doing whatever caught our attention at the time. It was so much fun.

The following week was my birthday. As many of my friends as possible took the night off. We rented a hotel room and secured plenty of pizza, liquor, and cake. At the time, I liked a particular brand of liquor that tasted just like fruit juice. I spent the entire night with a bottle in each hand—as if I could have drunk both bottles and lived! We weren't worried, because the camp was sending a van to pick us up at a specific time. We all went out to the parking lot to wait when Tate took me by the hand and led me across the parking lot behind a van. He started to kiss me and we had sex right there up against that van—with all of our friends only about fifty yards away. I must have worn a skirt that night. I got into the van to go back to camp in stunned silence. I couldn't help but wonder what that meant.

After that night, Tate and I began sleeping together again, but nothing about it was the same. The previous summer it had been great and wonderful and empowering. Now, I just felt like it was a chore and wanted to hurry up and get it over with.

Once camp was over, Audrey and I packed my car and headed home. The return home seemed *so* much longer than the drive to camp. Audrey was heartbroken about leaving Jay. I was heartbroken that Tate wasn't the man I thought he was. We were both completely exhausted. We were mostly quiet. We stopped in a hotel the first night. I don't remember how long the drive took, but as we neared Chicago, Audrey wanted to stop for the night. Chicago was less than two hours from home, so I wanted to push on. I couldn't wait to get home. Audrey was angry because she was ready to get out of the car. We made it to Wisconsin that night, and it was great to be home! I felt wrapped in the warmth of my family. Audrey had a couple of days to wait before her flight back home to Colorado, so we decided to take in some fun. We went to a giant theme park just south of Milwaukee. It was incredibly hot outside and we waited a long time in line for the first roller coaster. We finally were at the front of the line. The gate was right in front of me. The next thing I remembered was waking up on the platform, with medics taking my vitals and Audrey standing over me, looking worried. They took me to the first aid station and blamed the episode on heat stroke. I believed it was due to the migraines I'd experienced before camp. I didn't want to stay in the park and risk that happening again. We went to customer service to get refunds, but we were denied. The staff claimed we knew it was hot when we came to the theme park, so we were not entitled to refunds. I felt terrible and wanted to reimburse Audrey for her admission, but I didn't have the money. She flew out the next day. It was time for me to put childhood behind me and become an actual adult.

PART 3

A Rude Awakening

"No one saves us but ourselves. No one can and no one may.
We ourselves must walk the path." ~ **Buddha**

chapter 15

Time to Grow Up—or is It?

*I*n travel school, they offered us classes on every aspect of the travel industry, including how to secure a job. We were required to buy suits in either navy or black, create resumes, and practice our interviewing skills. That served me well. I researched the largest agency in my area and looked up the names I needed to know to get in the door. I put on my favorite suit (not the basic blue or black required in travel school, but black with a green-checkered jacket), put my resumes in a briefcase along with a notebook, and walked in the door and asked for the president by name. When they asked if I had an appointment, I said, "No, but he will want to see me." It *worked!* He came out to greet me, escorted me to his office and we chatted. He hired me on the spot and then introduced me to his hiring manager and announced that I'd just been added to the agency. For the second time, I sensed that I had gotten a job based on my looks, rather than my skills. But I intended to prove I was worth it by busting my butt on the job. At first, I thought I wanted to be a Leisure Travel Counselor, because it seemed Corporate Counselors were just order takers. They were always busy taking one call after another. In my work, I had time to get to know my clients, to probe their likes and dislikes, to offer options for a great vacation, and to arrange every detail throughout the trip. I eventually realized I was not suited to book vacation travel. I didn't like the things I had to learn about my clients. For example, one man asked me to book alternating trips—one with the girlfriend, one with the wife. I didn't like the elite and entitled attitude:

"You need to move us to another resort right now. My nanny doesn't like this one." And I came across arrogant people who would tell me just how important they were. They would drop my boss's name or say things like, "Do you know who I am?"

Eventually, I gravitated toward corporate travel. I moved out of our main call center and into our airport office. There, I did a little of everything—corporate, leisure, and travel documents. It was before the advent of electronic ticketing. We did all of the ticketing for the other offices when travelers wanted to pick their tickets up at the airport. I found that you could never escape the conceited crowd. I used to laugh at the guys who would rush in with ten minutes to flight time, pick up their tickets and say, "Call the gate and tell them to hold the flight." Yeah, right! I'm going to tell an airline to delay a departure and the other 200 people already on board because you were just too important to get there on time!

About that same time, a co-worker from the call center was looking for an additional roommate. I was anxious to move out of my parent's home and prove to the world that I was an adult. (Looking back, I was always a child in an adult environment. I just wanted to "fit in" and was hurt when I didn't. I spent far too much energy over far too many years trying to prove that I was an adult.) I agreed to share an apartment with two others, but about the time I moved in, roommate number two backed out. Now my rent would be a bit more than I expected. I was working two jobs, so I was sure I could handle it. I'd switched to being a cocktail waitress at the bowling alley and discovered I could make a *lot* more money during league play. I constantly walked around and interacted with the bowlers, making sure I spotted any empty glasses and offered refills. I consistently did twice the sales and made twice the tips of any other waitress who worked the same league. One waitress asked, "How come you always do so much more in sales than I do?" The answer was simple: She was reactive while I was proactive. She would just stand up by the counter and wait for a service light to come on. When I worked, no lights ever had to come on. The refills were already there. A short skirt never hurt either.

I moved into my new apartment in December 1990 at the age of 19.

It started out as so much fun! I didn't have to worry about anyone but me. If I wanted to stay out all night, I could. If I wanted to have a man spend the night, I could. Brandon and I picked up where we left off, which meant that we would occasionally go out or sleep together, but then he'd forget about plans we had made. I also slept occasionally with another bowling alley regular. One day when I was in the basement doing laundry, I met a guy who lived in the next building over. He was clearly hitting on me and told me to stop by his apartment. I did. We had amazing sex. Then he told me he had a girlfriend. Unbelievable! Despite that, I slept with him a few more times. Once was in the indoor pool. Now *that* was an experience, knowing someone could come through the door at any time! I'd learned what kind of car his girlfriend drove and would make myself crazy every time I saw it in the lot. I finally realized I was just an idiot and never saw him again.

Then Samantha pointed out a new bartender at work named Britt. She said, "I would sleep with him in a minute!" When I saw him, I said, "*A minute?* Damn! I would take him in .05 seconds!" As it turned out, the attraction was mutual. We went out a few times. We slept together a few times. Beyond his beautiful exterior, there wasn't much upstairs. Britt was then called up to the army during Operation Desert Storm. We weren't serious. In fact, I thought our relationship was pretty much over by the time he left. He wrote me a couple of letters when he was there. I wrote back. At one point I heard he was back in the States and was now engaged! I guess that would mean he must have been seeing his fiancée before he left. I felt betrayed, but I didn't really understand why.

Not long after moving into my apartment, I made friends with the neighbors upstairs, two single guys who were a lot of fun. My roommate was engaged to a man who was in a monastery to become a preacher. She had that "holier than thou" attitude. We didn't spend too much time together, because she was at her fiancée's place more often than not.

By this time, a number of us were transferred from one bowling alley to another within the chain. Sam and I would also go there to drink on a regular basis. We had some friends there from the previous location, and there were new friends to be made. I fell instantly in love with Christopher, a bartender at the new site! One night, when I was pretty drunk, I said to him, "I have to tell you something." Chris asked what it was. My romantic response was, "I think you're hotter than fuck!" He said thank you and then told me the feeling was mutual. That night Sam convinced Christopher's roommate, Randy, that we should all go to my apartment after leaving the bar. My roommate was out of town. So we went back to my apartment and drank beer. Eventually I asked if anyone wanted to see the indoor pool. Sam and Randy said no. Chris and I went for a walk to the pool. We started kissing sitting on the picnic table in the poolroom and things got really hot, really fast! Then he stopped me and said, "I'm not looking for a relationship." Despite the fact that I felt like I'd just been punched in the stomach, I smiled and said, "Who said anything about a relationship?" We picked up where we left off. We went back to the apartment and Sam and Randy left. Christopher and I went to my bedroom and had amazing, hot sex all night long. We tried positions that probably haven't been used in porn films.

The next morning I drove Chris home. He took my number and said he'd call me. I wasn't sure he would, but I was so excited when he called that night. He was bowling in a league with some of our friends and asked if I want to come and watch. Of course I did! From then on, I *thought* we'd started dating. We were constantly talking on the phone and sleeping at one another's apartments.

My roommate was getting married in July, and she told me that she planned to move out. I found a new roommate—my cousin Danielle. She had to be out of her place in April, so we moved her into my room until my roommate was ready to move out. Then, despite the amazingly large apartment we had with an indoor pool, my cousin said she wanted to find a cheaper place to live. So we looked for a new place and found one that would suffice. It lacked an indoor pool. It was your basic box apartment, but we each saved about $25 per month by moving! We signed the lease and planned to move in the following month. One night, Danielle and I came home to find that our roommate's family came for a visit. There was a mom, dad and six siblings! We retreated to our room and waited, for surely they would leave for their hotel soon. And then Danielle overheard that they all planned to sleep in *our* two-bedroom, one-bath apartment!

The first night, we went upstairs and hung out with the guys until it was time to go to bed. We just sat around drinking and talking. I was thinking about going back to school to become an emergency medical technician. One of the guys worked for the Milwaukee Fire Department, so he gave me his EMT study book. Danielle and I snuck in half drunk past all of the people sleeping in our living room and made it to our bedroom. When we asked her in the morning, our roommate said her family would be there for a couple more days! We both lost our composure and ended up staying at our respective parents' homes during that time.

After that episode, things were never the same. I ended up getting into an argument with my roommate when she switched all of the bills into my name without telling me. She also said her food was disappearing. I said, "I never eat your food!" She said, "Well, your cousin does." I was so furious with my roommate. She saw nothing wrong with having eight extra people stay in the apartment for four nights, but everything we said or did was wrong. We decided we were ready for our move. I called Christopher and he came over with his pick-up truck. Before long, we were at the new location. I had all of the utilities turned on at the new place, and I called and canceled all of the utilities that had been placed in my name at the first apartment. The last time I talked to my first roommate was when she called, furious because her electricity had just been turned off.

Christopher and I stayed close until late June when the entire group from the bar went to Milwaukee's Summerfest to watch me perform in the water ski show. After the show, I met up with the gang and found out that Chris had secured the phone number of a female bartender. I was devastated! I was sure that if we could spend more time together, then Chris would realize he loved me. For the rest of the year, we continued to sleep together whenever we ran into each other at the bar. Of course, I did my best to make sure this happened as often as possible.

That December, I drove over to my parent's house for groceries. I carried a bag out to the front porch, and I slipped on the ice. My left leg ended up behind me. My orthopedic doc wanted to care for it conservatively, because I'd already had two surgeries on that knee. I was put in a brace from hip to ankle. The following week, mom called me at work and said, "I think you should sue us." I didn't understand. *"What?"* She had already hired a lawyer for me, because Mom knew there was no way I could pay my household expenses—and the medical bills that were coming—while I was off my feet and not able to waitress. And we both knew I'd have to have surgery again. So, the lawsuit began.

Not long after my injury, I went down to Chicago to spend a weekend with Noah. I made that trip fairly often. Since my days at camp, every man I met was advised that if they couldn't handle me having Noah as a best friend, then they wouldn't have me at all. Meanwhile, Noah was either as blind as a bat or as dumb as a box of rocks, because I was in love with him for a couple of years but he never saw it. On this particular weekend, we went out with his older brother, Alan, who was attending law school. There seemed to be a certain attraction between us, and instead of going back to Noah's apartment that night, I went to Alan's. You can guess what happened next. I saw Alan a few times after that, and then the connection faded away. I never knew if it bothered Noah that I was seeing his brother, but I was glad I had stopped seeing him when I did. When I saw Alan years later at Noah's wedding, he was drunk and hit on me in front of his wife! His parents told him it was time for him to leave. How embarrassing.

Danielle and I settled into our apartment. We both went out drinking fairly often. Up to that point, I smoked occasionally when I was in a bar; Danielle smoked all of the time. It became a bonding experience between us. I would bum a cigarette from her and we would hang out watching TV. We actually didn't see each other all that much. When I wasn't at work, I was at the bar with my friends. She would often sleep at her boyfriend's house and Chris would sleep at our apartment whenever we ran into each other. I really thought Chris was "the one." He just hadn't figured that out yet. What I really noticed about Danielle was that she ate *everything* in the apartment! It made me crazy, because she was so thin and yet she could put more food away in one day than a normal person could in a week. It got so bad that I started keeping non-perishable foods like soup and boxed food in my trunk. I even tried hiding food under my bed, but she found it. One night, I went to the grocery store and spent $150 to stock up and have some food in the house, but by the time I got home from work the next day, it was *all gone!* I gave up. If I was hungry, I had two choices: I could go to the store and buy what I needed and then come home and cook it, or I could go get fast food at an assortment of drive-through restaurants near our apartment. When I look back on that year, it's a miracle I didn't gain 100 pounds! I drank heavily at least four nights a week, and ate out constantly. I finally had all I could take of Danielle.

chapter 16

Alone / Together

I really didn't want to find another roommate. I wanted a place of my own. Eventually, I found one that I could afford. By now I had finished EMT school. I worked at the travel agency by day and the ambulance company on nights and weekends. I also received a settlement from my knee injury that allowed me to pay the down payment for the new apartment. My money went pretty fast once I paid all of my bills and debts, but I was still able to splurge on a new bathroom set in light blue.

I loved my first "alone" apartment! I was still on the wild side. One night I went to a local church festival and ran into a guy, Kendall, who had been a senior when I was a freshman. In high school, he was captain of the baseball and basketball teams, and he wanted to meet me. We were introduced at a dance and we shared the dance floor during a couple of songs. That was it. I hadn't given him my number and it took me too long to decide whether I wanted to date him. By then, he had begun dating someone else.

So on that night, years later when I ran into him, Kendall followed me home from the festival. I told him he could park next to me as the downstairs neighbor didn't have a car. So imagine my shock and surprise when I began to pull in and found Brandon parked in my spot, sleeping in his car! I told Kendall that the neighbors must have company and asked him to park around front. As soon as he pulled away, I knocked on Brandon's window and he startled awake. I said, "What are you doing here?" He replied, "Waiting for you!" I said, "You can't be here. I have company!"

He just said, "Oh," put the car in reverse, and then he drove away. I met Kendall in the yard and we went upstairs to my apartment. I had no doubt where this was going, so I made no small talk. I started kissing him and we got down to business. When we were done, he apologized. I asked why and he said he hadn't intended for things to go that far. I didn't really believe or understand that at all. In my mind, whenever a man came to a woman's house, or vice versa, the end game was always sex.

In the short time I'd been in that apartment, Chris had come over once or twice, Brandon had come over once, and a nameless guy spent the night of my 21st birthday in my bed. It was all pretty crazy.

One day I was home for the weekend when Sam called me from Green Bay. The pro bowler's tour was there and they were having so much fun. She said I should come up. And so I drove up to Green Bay. I met a bowler named Tim, whom all of my friends at our home bowling alley always talked about as a friend. I was surprised, because even though he was 30 and I was all of 20ish, he was cute and fun. He was obviously flirting with me and catered to my every whim. I'd recently had knee surgery, so he picked me up and carried me as we walked from one bar to the next. I saw a horse-drawn carriage and said, "Awww," and the next thing you know, I was sitting next to Tim in the carriage. We flirted all night. I always checked for wedding rings, and he most definitely was *not* wearing one. When we were finally alone in the ladies room, I said, "Sam, you didn't tell me Tim was totally hot!" She said, "I guess I didn't tell you he's married either." Oh *shit!* I had already fallen for this guy and *now* she tells me he's married! I was really torn. The chemistry between us was undeniable. But up to that point, I'd never slept with a married man. Sam did a while back, and I expressed my disapproval. Now here I was considering a visit to Tim's hotel room instead of the one Sam and I were sharing. That night, I crossed a line that I could never uncross. I slept with Tim. It was amazing. Of course, he told me all of the things I needed to hear, like "my marriage is not happy" and "we haven't been sleeping together for a long time," and all of the other lies a married guy says to justify an affair.

Tim continued to call me whenever he was going to be in the area, and we got together. The following year, when the tour was returning to Green Bay, I was excited at the prospect of spending the weekend together.

The last thing I expected was the way things turned out. In the bar that night, Tim was like a butterfly, stopping to talk to everyone except me. Somehow I knew he'd still be with me when the night was over. That was the night Tim told me that he and his wife had gone to a fertility clinic and were trying to have a baby. I had never been so stunned in my life. He had just had sex with me and was now telling me this! He always told me what a shrew she was and how they were heading for divorce. Obviously, that wasn't the case. Any illusions I had about him were shattered. I was "the other woman." I felt so dirty.

The next day was *huge*. Tim had bowled his way into the top five of the tournament, which meant he would appear on the television broadcast. A new young bowler named Devin also made the top five. Tim had arranged to give Devin a ride to the bowling alley, supporting him as he prepared for his first TV appearance. Devin was very nice to look at from behind, and Sam could not stop talking about him. When the match was over, we all went back to the bar—and Devin expressed his interest in me.

chapter 17

I'm Not Sure if I Do

I don't even remember if we so much as kissed that weekend, but things with Devin got very serious very fast! Because he was on the road every week, it didn't make sense to get him his own apartment in Milwaukee. We decided he should move into mine. My mother was even so helpful as to send a folding bed for my second bedroom so he would have somewhere to sleep. Oh my!

Our life together was *far* from normal. By now I was working 24-hour shifts at the ambulance company and just an occasional weekend for the travel agency. I always had free airline tickets to use and my 24-hour schedule allowed me to be off five days in a row every third week. On those weeks, I would fly to wherever Devin was bowling. I became used to staying in hotels, sending out laundry, eating out every day and night, and sitting in a bowling center all day long.

Devin and I had only been together for about five months or so when Sam and I planned a trip to Vegas to meet his family. We had barely gotten into the house—and I was still absorbing names and my environment—when I realized that Devin was on his knee and was presenting me with a *huge* diamond ring. I said, "Yes!" I had no idea this was going to happen, or that he had this incredible ring for me! It turned out that the diamond had been in his family. We set a wedding date and the planning began. We would have a large wedding in November when bowling season was on a break. It would be in Milwaukee.

Six weeks before the wedding, everything was set. The invitations had just gone out, and the bridesmaids and I had our dresses. My friend Jody was in town from Minneapolis for her final dress fitting. The ambulance company had its annual picnic that day. My friend from work, Dave, met Jody the last time she'd been in town, and they had hit it off. Dave lived more than an hour from where we worked, so the plan was for the two of them to spend the night at my apartment. The picnic started early and we had a blast. Throughout the day, a thought kept popping into my head: "I'm having so much fun. I'm glad Devin's not here or it wouldn't be fun." Devin was known to mope, make fun of me, or throw temper tantrums when we were out. This was a *huge* red flag to me. How could I be marrying this man in less than two months when I'm thankful he's not here, instead of wishing he were.

We drank all day and ended the night at a bar only a few blocks from my apartment. One of the guys from work, Paul, walked us out of the bar. He leaned in and kissed me goodnight, and I kissed back! What kind of woman does that? The kind who's miserable in her relationship. This was eye-opening for me. I already knew I couldn't marry Devin, but I was afraid to say it out loud. For weeks, I had confided my feelings to friends, mostly Sam. I was looking for someone to tell me I was right, that we weren't compatible. Or that I should follow my gut: If I wasn't 100 percent sure I loved him, then I should wait. Instead, Sam told me how incredibly lucky I was to have such a great guy who wanted to marry me. When Dave, Jody, and I walked into the apartment at bar time, the phone rang. It was Devin—and he was itching for a fight. He got one. He had been jealous of Dave for some time. Dave was my partner at work and we had quickly become great friends.

When I answered the phone, Devin said, "Are you just getting home?" I said yes, and that Dave and Jody were in the other room. He asked when I decided to have Dave spend the night. Was it as soon as I found out he would be out of town that weekend? I was so furious that I said: "Yes. That's exactly what I did. I called him and said, 'Hey Dave, Devin is going to be out of town next weekend. Do you want to come over so we can fuck?'" Our phone conversation went downhill from there. I knew that if Devin didn't trust me, it would never work. We argued for at least 30 minutes. When I hung up the phone, I joined Dave and Jody and said, "I can't do it." Dave said, "You can't do what?" I said, "I can't marry him." Dave put a hand on my shoulder and said, "Bridgette, you've had an awful lot to drink today to be making that kind of decision. Maybe you should go to sleep and see how you feel about it in the morning." I agreed and went to my room. I was terrified that I was only able to voice my true feelings because I was drunk. I was afraid that, in the light of morning, the pressure of 250 invitations, hall, catering, dresses, etc., would crash back down on me and I wouldn't be able to put an end to it.

Dave had to work in the morning. Before he left, he stopped in my room and sat down on my bed. He said, "How do you feel this morning?" I said, "I still can't do it." Jody then revealed that my surprise bridal shower was planned today. Oh crap! It was only hours away. I immediately tried to call my mother, but she wasn't home. I called my sister-in-law and told her I knew my shower was supposed to be today, but I was not going to marry Devin. It was too late. I had to go to my surprise shower and tell everyone to enjoy the food, but there would be no wedding. I remember watching them all leave with their gifts. One kind woman gave me her gift and told me she still wanted me to have it. It was a set of towels—and I never forgot her kindness.

That night when Devin came home, the first thing he did was look at my ring finger and saw that I wasn't wearing the ring. The next week was pretty much a blur. Devin had to stay until his parents drove a van from Vegas to help him move his stuff back. We went together to the jewelry store to return our wedding rings. *That* really threw the clerk for a loop. My parents and I sent postcards to everyone who was given an invite, informing them that the wedding was canceled. My parents paid all of my bridesmaids for their dresses. They were so wonderful and supportive. And I felt like such a loser. How could I have planned such a big wedding to a man who I'd never seen laugh unless it was at my expense. I felt like a child again.

Samantha took the news of our breakup *very* hard. It was clear that she was siding with Devin and would follow him around. I ended up losing both my fiancé and my best friend at the same time. That was hard to take. A few months after what would have been our wedding day, Sam confessed to me that she had slept with Devin that night. That effectively ended our friendship.

chapter 18

Repairing the Damage

I was lucky that the people who worked with me at the ambulance company were *very* social. I worked a *ton* of hours and became good friends with many of them. Around this time, my youngest brother Rodney and his wife, Marie, approached me with an offer. They had moved up to their lake house and their other house had been empty and on the market for a year. They asked if I wanted to move into it. I did! It was only four houses down from where my parents lived—and it was a real house. I invited a guy from the ambulance company, named Steve, to be a roommate. He was exactly what I needed at that time. He just returned to work after taking some time off, and I didn't really know him. He was a "surfer dude" in a city that didn't have much surf. He slept in one of the upstairs bedrooms, while I settled into the master bedroom downstairs. He refused to let me sit at home and feel sorry for myself. Nope! We would either walk down to the corner pub to have a beer together or he would take me out with our co-workers to some of the more popular clubs. He was good for me at that time. Surprisingly, Steve told me one day that he had to report to jail to serve 30 days on a traffic violation. I wasn't worried. He called me from jail and told me he felt like such a loser, and he asked if I still wanted him as a roommate. I said, "Of course, but the house just sold so I have to find us a two-bedroom apartment." He said, "Okay." He trusted me. I found a great little apartment and signed the lease. I never heard from Steve again. Despite my repeated attempts to contact him, I was left with a clothes basket, one box of his junk, and a lease on a two-

78

bedroom apartment when I needed only one. About a month after I moved in, Dave explained that he had to be out of his apartment by the weekend and that his new roommate had just backed out on him. He knew I had an extra room and, after a brief hesitation, I said, "Okay, but just for the month!"

Months later, Dave and I were the best set of roommates ever, except when I had female friends from out of town sleeping over. Somehow, they always ended up sleeping in Dave's room. But that was okay, as long as everyone was happy. We became the best of friends. We worked together, and then we came home and played video games for hours. Eventually, one of us would get up and make dinner. We laughed at the same things, over and over. A movie—*Son in Law,* featuring Pauly Shore—came out at that time, and it was so stupidly funny. We watched it repeatedly. We loved the part when Pauly's character walked into the dorm hallway wearing Thanksgiving pajamas, and said, "Becca, Steven Tyler PJs!" Dave and I said that to each other all the time, and then we laughed and laughed.

One morning, after the two of us just got off of a 24-hour shift, Dave talked me into dropping in at a bar, one that was patronized by cops, firefighters, and emergency medical technicians. We stopped for only one drink. That was when we learned that not only was it Opening Day for the Milwaukee Brewers, but the bus was leaving in one hour, and tickets were still available. Dave begged me to go for it. We went home to change and returned to the bar in time to board the bus. It was *so* cold, and I was so tired from having just finished a long shift at work! We passed bottles of liquor to keep warm. At the game, I was freezing. Around the fourth inning, I decided to go back to the bus. I crawled up onto the luggage rack and took a nice long nap until the end of the game. Everyone may have given me a hard time for it, but the nap was refreshing and it allowed me to keep hanging out with everyone when we got back.

One day I ran into an old "friend" at that same bar—Britt, that cute bowling alley bartender who joined the army during Operation Desert Storm and was now a county sheriff. Before he inserted himself into my conversation, I was talking with a cute paramedic who had boyfriend potential. Britt was a very large man, and sadly, he made it clear to everyone in shouting distance that I was off limits. He told me that things could have worked out for us, but I was just too wild for him. Britt was still married, but he wanted to take me home. We went round and round for hours. He wouldn't take no for an answer. Eventually I gave in and let him come home with me. This was the second time that I knowingly broke that cardinal law about married men. It wasn't even worth it. I didn't want to insult him, but he wasn't nearly as good as he thought he was. Instead of satisfied, I just felt dirty.

chapter 19

Would've, Should've, Could've

Dave and I lived together in perfect harmony for quite a while. Six months or so after my would-have-been wedding, my boss at the ambulance company, Josh, began to call me to his office more and more often to "talk." By now, I had been the shift supervisor for two or three years. At first, the talk was always about work. What did I think about the performance of this employee? What were my thoughts on the new equipment? Eventually, he began to talk to me about his marriage. He told me how unhappy he was, saying he didn't know how to fix the relationship. I was naïve enough to believe he was asking for my help. I suggested counseling, roses, and weekend getaways. Hell, I'd never been married! Why would this man, who was ten years older than me, ask *me* for marriage advice? It became clear that he had given up on his marriage. He said he'd asked for a divorce. Then he asked if we could go out for a beer. I was leery. We proceeded to have a four-hour conversation just on the implications of us going out for a beer. Josh said he was staying with a mutual friend. But somehow or other, I knew that once I went for that beer, my fate would be sealed. It would either be the end of my career or the beginning of a long-term relationship.

It turned out to be the beginning of a long-term relationship. We went out once or twice for dinner. We slept together once or twice, and then Josh moved himself into my place. Dave was really upset that I didn't tell him right away when things between Josh and me started. I didn't want to risk the news getting out at work. Stupid me! If I had only told Dave, he wouldn't have said anything. But, since I didn't tell him, he gossiped with the rest of them. Our living situation quickly became unmanageable. Josh was jealous of my arrangement with Dave and did everything possible to drive a wedge between us. He thought it was inappropriate that Dave sat around in boxer shorts. I told him that Dave went to the store in his boxer shorts. Josh thought it was inappropriate that one of us would brush our teeth in the bathroom sink while the other was in the shower. It wasn't like you could see anything!

Soon Josh found himself a duplex owned by one of our co-workers to move into. Unfortunately, he had absolutely *no* means to support himself. I ended up buying necessities for him on my credit card. I began to spend most of my time with Josh, so I brought my cat to his house. And then I moved in with him. Most of our furniture consisted of items Josh was "storing" for Mark, a mutual friend who had moved back home temporarily. At night, we used a sleeper sofa in the living room. That same friend soon gave Josh a waterbed frame, and we bought a mattress for it. We moved my full-size bed into the second bedroom for when Josh's children came to visit. We became engaged on December 23, 1994.

One of my biggest regrets is that I didn't stay in contact with Dave after I moved out. I don't know if he found a roommate and stayed there, or if he moved somewhere else. He and I completely lost touch. Josh and I were married in November 1995. Dave didn't even attend our wedding. I had allowed Josh to convince me that my best friend had turned against me by spreading rumors at work. It's hard, now, to imagine that I was so easily manipulated, considering how jaded I had already become. But I was truly in love with the idea of being in love. I wanted that suburban American life with a husband, kids, and a white picket fence.

By the time the wedding was growing near, I already had secret doubts, but I would *not* be labeled as "The Runaway Bride." I had fallen madly in love with Josh's two children and did *not* want to disappoint them. I also didn't want to disappoint my family, which strongly disapproved of me moving in with Josh when I did. I wanted to prove to the world that Josh and I were not just a "flash in the pan" and that I was not just a "rebound girl." If I had understood back then that I could do what was best for me and not care what others thought, I'm certain I would have run the other way.

Josh and I knew we could not continue our current working situation. He was my boss and I was the direct supervisor of everyone working my shift. We instructed the employees that they were to go to the vice president of the company if they had any issues with me, my performance, or Josh. And then both of us changed jobs. Around the time of our marriage, Josh began working in the service department of a car dealership with my brother Rodney. It paid almost twice what he had been making. I accepted a new job in a local hospital, working as an anesthesia technician. The job provided me more normal hours (with the exception of on-call shifts) and paid about $4 more per hour than I had been making. In theory, we should be doing pretty well—but we never were. When the time came when we had to return the furniture we'd been using to our friend Mark, we were forced to come up with a plan. Josh didn't want the used furniture that I had stored in the apartment's garage. He wanted new. We didn't qualify for credit at the large furniture store in town, so we ordered through Fingerhut. I was shocked when the furniture arrived, because it wasn't what I had picked out with Josh. (He told me that what we planned to get was on back order, so he chose alternative items himself.) I'm also sure we paid much more than we should have. At this point, I still trusted him and didn't really question it further. He repeatedly asked me to trust him when it came to the checkbook and paying bills, but somehow we were always bouncing checks. Overdraft fees kept piling up. We had great difficulty paying our bills. I had run up large balances on my credit cards helping Josh set up a household. We ended up relying on a Credit Counseling Agency to consolidate our debt and help us make affordable monthly payments.

chapter 20

Far from Home and All Alone

Not long after we were married, we moved to a suburb about thirty miles north of where I had lived my entire life. Although I didn't want to leave the area I'd grown up in and where my family was, I knew we had to do what was right by Josh's children. If they were going to spend time with us, we needed to be near their schools and friends. We found a nice three-bedroom upper duplex that was *very* reasonable. The only catch was that we would be responsible for mowing grass and plowing snow, as the homeowner was an 89-year-old woman who lived downstairs. It was a cute place and I loved it. It also was close enough so I could respond quickly when I was needed at the hospital. I slept in my clothes when I was on call so I could get up and run out the door to work. I actually *hated* my job.

Working at the hospital was the first job in my life that I neither liked nor was successful at. I should have asked more questions during the interview process, such as, "Why do you suddenly have to fill five positions?" The fact that everyone had quit before I was hired should have been a red flag, but I was convinced that I was stronger, smarter, and more determined than everybody else. Unfortunately, those traits had nothing to do with success in this particular job. Because everyone before me had left, nobody was there to help me learn the job. Three of us were hired at the same time. Our principal responsibility was easy enough: checking the anesthesia carts and equipment. After that, everything got blurry. We assisted thirteen different anesthesiologists, and each of them wanted things done a different way—and each surgery required different equipment and positioning of patients. *That* depended upon which doctor was doing the surgery. Cardiac surgery was the most difficult. Three of us were hired simultaneously, but only one technician could be trained at a time in open-heart surgery. I was the last. By the time I began training in the cardiac room, I had been there long enough that the anesthesiologists expected me to already know what to do. But I hadn't had the opportunity to even observe in the cardiac room until then. One anesthesiologist used drugs and methods that were dated, and she covered her incompetence with arrogance. I was shocked at the number of people who had such great respect for her skill, when I could see clearly that she was about a decade behind the other cardiac anesthesiologists. Every time I was on her service, she would yell, belittle, and berate me in front of an entire operating room filled with people. I began to imagine being carjacked on my way to work every morning, and I was always disappointed when I arrived safely at work with no excuse to not be there. After eight months at that job, I reached out to one of my former contacts in the travel business. She set me up with an interview with one of her employees. I interviewed for a corporate travel position with American Express and was offered the job.

I would have to take a slight pay cut, but it would be worth it to not cry on my way to work anymore. I also joined the local volunteer fire department as an EMT so that I could still have my "trauma fix."

Once I started at American Express, I quickly drew the attention of my boss and co-workers. Nobody expected me to pick up the computer system and account information as quickly as I did. The company gave an annual award to the top 5 percent of all employees. Because I started working there in September 1996, I wasn't eligible for the award that year, but I made it clear to my boss that I would win it the next year. I also told her that I expected to be promoted as her equal within the next year. Instead of laughing at me or brushing me off, she took me seriously and helped me work toward my goals. Within the first six months, I was able to do international reservations and handle VIP callers. About that same time, my husband called me at work to say he'd been fired from his job. I was a total wreck!

When I arrived home from work to discuss the situation, Josh told me his version of what happened. He tried to make it *seem* like the world was against him. He said the car dealership planned to fight his unemployment claim by saying he had quit his job, when he actually was fired. But Josh didn't even file for unemployment. My brother Rodney, who had worked at the dealership for many years, told me that Josh quit his job. This was the first time Josh told me an outright lie since we had been married. I quickly realized that I couldn't question him, because his temper frightened me enough to back off. Josh spent the next six months supposedly looking for work, but I didn't see him trying at all. I saw him sitting on his ass telling me why every job was beneath him. I tried to make him see that *any* job would bring some money into the household. We were going under fast. Josh accepted a bartending job, but he showed up for one shift before deciding it wasn't for him. As my career began to soar, Josh's self-esteem began to nosedive. His temper—and what I now recognize as verbal abuse—began to erupt more frequently.

Eventually, Josh took a job as a mover. The money wasn't great, but at least he was contributing *something*. We often argued about money. During one argument, he punched a hole into a plaster wall right next to my head. I knew at that moment that one day, some day, Josh would strike me. I told him it was my "line in the sand." If he ever struck me, I would be out the door before he knew what hit him. As our financial problems escalated, Josh suggested that we file for bankruptcy. I was against it. I knew he had done that in his previous marriage, but he had convinced me that his ex-wife was at fault. Now I began to see it was a part of who he was. He bounced check after check. Overdraft and late fees pulled us further and further down. We hired a lawyer and filed for a chapter 13 bankruptcy to help us consolidate our debt. It was horribly embarrassing, but necessary. We started paying back what we owed in monthly payments. A few months later, Josh pushed me to file for chapter 7 bankruptcy, which would eliminate our debt but subject us to losing property not exempt from collection. I was against this plan, as well, but I didn't see a choice. Finally, I agreed. Josh had been in and out of at least eight jobs by then.

One day, out of the blue, Josh was determined to move into a townhouse that cost $150 per month more than what we were paying. I now think he wanted to move because he hadn't paid our rent. He thought fixing a retaining wall in the yard would cover our rent that month, but he never discussed it with our landlord. He also tried to fix the bathroom wall after I put my foot through it while taking a bath. He did *not* find the source of the water leak that caused drywall rot. He just added a patch of drywall and covered it with tiles. It looked horrible.

My most enlightening moment occurred one day as I listened to Josh talking on the phone with the rental company after we'd been declined for the more expensive townhouse, due to our credit history. He had his best "salesman" voice on. By now, I recognized that voice and couldn't believe people actually fell for it. (And yet, I'd fallen for it for years as we worked together, even before we began dating.) Josh told the rental company that he wanted a chance to explain why we filed for bankruptcy, out of no fault of our own. I whipped my head around to look at him. I wanted to scream, "Who the hell's fault do you think it was? We bought stuff we couldn't afford and you quit your job! How is any of that not our fault?" Somehow, his line worked. We were approved for the townhouse. I felt like he screwed our landlord, a nice old lady, out of money due. I wanted to go back and give it to her myself, but I didn't have any money of my own.

Not too long after we moved into the townhouse, Noah wanted to ride up on his motorcycle to introduce me to his girlfriend, Judy. Noah and I had remained close throughout our wild years, and we were still close. Noah's previous girlfriend didn't impress me, and didn't expect much with the new one. When they arrived, I had to run to the store for something and Judy immediately volunteered to go with me. With that simple gesture, she won my approval. She was kind and sweet. I wanted to hate her, because I hadn't completely gotten over Noah, but I loved her and thought she was perfect for him. Not to mention, I was married. (Deep down, I already suspected it wouldn't last forever.)

Josh maintained complete control of our money. He always told me that he paid the bills, but I kept taking calls from collection agencies saying the bills weren't paid. Whenever I questioned him, his temper flared. At one point, after I took the checkbook and his ATM card from him, Josh found a box of blank checks in a drawer and began writing them. He got home before I did and hid the overdraft notices. I never bought anything unless I had cash, so that I would be spared the embarrassment of a clerk saying we had bounced a check there. In the four years we were married, things kept going downhill. While my career continued to improve and soar, Josh kept moving from one job to the next. Surprisingly, he stuck with one of his jobs, one that paid very well, for nearly a year. Our outlook looked encouraging. Josh had a vasectomy during his first marriage, but he knew I wanted kids of my own. We saw a fertility doctor about artificial insemination. The procedure required pills to be taken three or four days prior to the insemination. On the day I brought home the pills, Josh came home and was excited to tell me that he just quit his great job and had taken a $10 per hour factory job, because it would be more fun and closer to home. I threw the pills out. I became more and more depressed. All I could see in my future was darkness. Josh and I simply sat around the house and ate and smoked cigarettes. In the span of our marriage of four years, I had gone from being well-toned and beautiful to fat and broken. When Josh's kids were with us, I did what I could to help them with homework. I sang them to sleep every night. I did my best to stay in the marriage for their sake. My heart broke every time I heard Josh make a promise to them that I knew we couldn't keep. Then, in one single night, the walls came crashing down.

chapter 21

The Line in the Sand

Josh and I joined a gym together and we agreed to quit smoking. We made a pact that if one of us were unable to quit, there would be no more smoking in the house. I started going to the gym daily. Josh went for a few weeks and then quit—as he did with just about everything in his life. I was able to quit smoking. The weight started to come off and my confidence returned. One night, before I left to drive Josh's daughter, Amelia, to a school dance, I went upstairs to tell him that we were leaving. When I knocked and opened the bathroom door, Josh had his razor in one hand and a lit cigarette in the other. The look on my face must have been one of horror. I said, "I thought we said no smoking!" Josh replied, "Well, it was only in the house." I said, "This *is* the house!" He grabbed me by the shoulders, threw me through the open bathroom door, through the open bedroom door, across the bedroom and into the chest. He immediately knew he'd crossed the line. I put on my happy face while I drove his daughter to school. As I dropped her off, I told her how much I loved her. I cried when she got out of the car, because I knew I would not be there when she got home. I went home and began packing my bags. Josh tried to stop me. He tried to talk me out of leaving. He called our friends and asked them to talk to me. He even called my brother Rodney, thinking he would talk me out of leaving. Instead, my brother told me to come and stay with him.

I stayed with Rodney and his family for a couple of days. I didn't know if I wanted to try and save my marriage or just cut and run. Even though we had already tried marriage counseling, I refused to come home until we got some more. Josh supposedly called the priest at the Catholic Church we attended only a few times. He said the priest couldn't meet with us until late the following week. I didn't want to be in limbo that long. A good friend of ours called and said her pastor would see us immediately. We met with her and came to some terms that allowed me to come home. However, for the next couple of weeks all I thought was, "I want out!" Josh's parents had gone to Arizona for the winter, so I knew he had a place to go. I finally mustered up the courage and said, "I want a divorce. I need you to pack your things and go stay at your parents' house until we can figure things out." Once those words were out of my mouth, the world had color again. The weight was lifted off of my shoulders. I had potential for happiness in my future!

I was so relieved to be on the path of divorce that there were no words to express it. However, I was terrified to tell my parents. I came from a large Catholic family, and people just didn't get divorced. Three of my four brothers had been married for many years. I called my mother. When she answered the phone, I said, "Mom, I need to tell you something. I've asked Josh for a divorce." As I waited for that bomb to settle in, Mom went on as if she hadn't even heard me. She said, "Okay, honey, but I have some bad news. Your father has a tumor." I sat down on the couch as if the floor had just fallen out from under me. She explained the nature of my dad's cancer and told me about the surgery that was scheduled to remove it.

I just sat there. On what I considered the most difficult night of my life, I wondered, "What is someone supposed to do at a time like this? Should I call a friend? Watch mindless TV while eating ice cream? Or maybe I should get out to the gym." I settled on the gym, which by now was a second home to me. I knew most of the people there, and that, in itself, was solace. That night I bench-pressed until my arms were rubber and my chest was burning. Then I did an hour of cardio exercises.

Dad had his surgery. The surgeons removed the entire tumor and they did not believe it had spread. My parents looked at apartments with me and put down a deposit on one we agreed upon. I elected to stay in the town where Josh and I lived, because it had become home and I'd been on the fire department for over three years. Josh accused me of taking all of his options. HE wanted that apartment. HE wanted to join the fire department (which he had already done once and then backed out). In the end, I moved into my new apartment and my mother did an incredible job of securing secondhand furnishings for me. Josh and I split up most of our belongings. I insisted he keep the living room set, because I always hated it and it smelled like smoke. I took the bedroom set.

PART 4

Stepping Out

"The best protection any woman can have is courage."
~ Elizabeth Cady Stanton

chapter 22

Born Again!

I moved into my new apartment on October 30, 1999. I spent New Year's Eve with Noah. We planned to have a poker party. By now, he and Judy had bought a house together, but she was out of town for the holidays. Noah pulled out a ring box to show me, as he was about to propose to Judy. I was both thrilled and crushed at the same time. I knew she was "the one" for him, but I still loved him. Our timing was just poor! I was truly happy for him. Judy was the kind of woman you would just love to hate, because she has everything you've ever wanted in life. But you can't hate her, because she is one of the most genuine and kind people you've ever met. And a dozen years later, she still is! She always was "the one" for Noah. They have three beautiful children and she is an incredible stay-at-home mom! She gives Noah the freedom that a lot of wives would resent. He still plays poker and softball after work, and continues to buy and renovate properties.

I began to become friends with a woman named Christine who worked in the same office I did. Christine's wardrobe seemed suited for "Little House on the Prairie," but she was *really* good at her job. When I received a promotion as Call Center Team Leader, she was the customer service representative. We didn't seem to have much in common, but Christine had a daughter who was the same age as Josh's daughter Amelia. They went to same school together and occasionally hung out. One day in January, in the office lunchroom, Christine said to me, "I don't know you well enough. If I know something about your ex-husband, do you want to know?" I said sure. She told me that her daughter had gone to Amelia's birthday party in January. At that party, Josh proposed to his new "roommate." It took him less than three months to meet someone and propose. If only I'd known five years ago how co-dependent he was! People asked me if I thought Josh cheated on me with his new fiancée. I knew he didn't, because he didn't meet her until after we had separated, when he went back to work at the ambulance company. In the end it didn't matter. Our lives were separate!

Josh's new fiancée may have saved my life. One night, shortly after we split up and I still lived in the townhouse, I was called out on a rescue in the middle of the night. Returning home about 3:00 a.m., I saw Josh walking across a bridge about a block from the townhouse. I stopped and asked what he was doing. His said he was walking back to his parents' house. He told me he'd been sitting in a parking lot watching the townhouse when his car died. I offered him a ride. Looking back at it now, I'm lucky that act of kindness on my behalf didn't result in violent consequences. And I can't believe I didn't panic at the thought that Josh was watching my house in the middle of the night! I am thankful he met his third wife right away or things could have turned ugly.

I became great friends with Christine and many of the people from the fire department and the gym. In March, I threw a "Divorce Party" to celebrate the official end of my marriage, and I invited many people from the office and the fire department. We had a great time!

Not long after my divorce, I tried out my single girl sexual wings again. I attended a birthday party for the sister of some firefighter friends. I met a guy there and he came home with me that night. It wasn't a good experience, but it at least made me feel like I was desirable again.

Christine and I started going out together when we could. She was a single parent, and her daughter was still too young to be left home alone. We went out whenever her daughter had a sleepover with friends. The *real* Christine was *so* different than the one I'd met in the office. She was fun, wild, and outgoing. She traded what I thought of as her "Little House on the Prairie" clothing for leopard print shirts, short skirts and heels. She randomly grabbed cute guys as they walked by and they stopped to talk with us. She also said things like, "We need to find a different bar. We're not getting enough attention here." That was one of the first times in my life when it became acceptable to "want attention" and say so.

With Christine's help, I re-established a sense of style and continued my transformation from ugly duckling to swan. (I felt very undesirable while married. I was fat, never wore make up, couldn't afford decent clothes, and always had *really bad* haircuts!) I went from being dependent on someone else for everything to being confident and competent. That was who I'd been before Josh wore me down and who I fully intended to return to.

I also became good friends with a young woman from the rescue squad named Hannah. She and I often talked on the phone during my first few months as a single woman. One night, while we were talking on the phone, I heard her say, "*Ouch!* That had to hurt!" When I asked what she was watching, she said bull riding. I had never seen it before. I flipped to the channel she was watching, just in time to see the instant replay. The emergency medical technician in me was thinking, "*Wow!* I'd do this, splint that, and immobilize just about everything before moving him." A doctor serving the arena quickly went to the side of the fallen bull rider, asked him a couple of questions, and suddenly the cowboy was standing up and walking with assistance in almost no time at all. This scene completely fascinated me. I began watching bull riding on TV every chance I got. I decided I wanted see it live, and I told Christine about my wish.

chapter 23

Bull What?

Christine was about as female as any woman could possibly be. She knew absolutely nothing about sports, much less bull riding! She thought I was nuts, but simply said, "If you're going to make me watch bull riding, we're at least going to a city I like." A few weeks later, we were Houston bound! Those were the days when working in the travel industry still included perks like free airline tickets. Between the two of us, we'd built up a good stash of them. To book the hotel, I went directly through the travel agency for the Professional Bull Riders. That meant we would be staying at the same hotel with all of the tough guys I'd been watching so closely on TV! From the moment we stepped into the hotel, Christine decided maybe bull riding wasn't such a bad sport to watch. Sitting on a bench right in front of the doors was a cowboy with the most incredible blue eyes I'd ever seen. The lobby was filled with cowboys everywhere! That weekend, we met a number of the guys and even hung out with them a bit. Knowing the cowboys made watching bull riding on TV that much more exciting. Christine and I became avid fans. We began going to a number of tour stops each year. Every time we went, we met with and partied with a number of cowboys. I had developed an extreme crush on one of them and even had him pose with me while Christine took the picture.

Christine and I soon realized that the most fun we had was hanging out with the guys in the hotel lobby after the post-event party. We began to bring drinks and snacks and hang out in the lobby. As the guys trickled back into the hotel after their event, they would always stop by to hang out with us. We met more and more cowboys and began to go to more and more events. After a while, hotels wouldn't allow us to linger in the lobby all night, so it became widely known that if the Wisconsin girls were at an event, there would be an "after" party in their room.

The most memorable of those parties occurred in Grand Rapids, Michigan. We brought a girlfriend, Shelly, from the fire department, with us to that event—and she loved it. The three of us crashed the post-event party at a bar across from the hotel where we were socializing. We wrote our room number with a Sharpie on the hands of anyone we wanted to come to our party. I also spent time at the bar doing shots with my cowboy crush. As we left for our hotel room, Shelly and Christine told me that I had probably overindulged at the bar and should cool off a bit. I thought, "Oh shit! All of these cowboys are coming to our room for a party and I'm completely drunk!" (Being around a man I absolutely idolized and buying him shots had something to do with that!) We returned to our room and Christine and Shelly began to set out beverages and snacks. I went into the bathroom, hoping to make myself vomit. I had just gotten down on my knees in front of the toilet when my "Dream Cowboy" came crashing into our hotel room and then into the bathroom, where he began yelling, *"You're puking!"* I immediately stood up and said I had been looking for an earring (as if *anybody* would believe me considering the condition I was in). Sadly, it was one of the best parties in history and I was in no condition to socialize. At one point, I passed out in a corner chair. But every once in a while, I woke up and looked around the room and marveled at the number of people in our room. There were some *very* famous people there!

When I woke up in the morning and looked around the room, I was completely astonished at what I saw. There was not an inch of our room that wasn't covered in chips, beer cans, beer bottles, and wine bottles! While Christine and Shelly began to pick up, I went into the hallway to find our maid. I handed her a $20 bill and said, "I am *so* sorry." I went back in to help clean up. Underneath the carpet of chips was a man's wedding ring. We had no way of knowing who it belonged to. Throughout the rest of the weekend, every time one of us put on a pair of shoes or boots, they always contained chips.

The following night, we decided we would *not* host a party, as it had gotten out of hand the night before. We invited only three or four cowboys who we'd clicked with. First, however, I went to the bar and approached the president of the Bull Rider's Association and said, "I need to talk to you." I wanted to get him away from his entourage of followers. I said, "You know that party we had last night?" He said, "Yeah." I handed him the ring and said, "Someone appears to have lost this. Can you please find him and return it?" He assured me he would. Just after bar time, a knock sounded on our hotel room door. I expected it to be the cowboys we invited over. I opened the door, only to be surprised by the president with his entourage. I explained that we were not hosting a party that night. He said, "Well, you'd better tell that to the lobby, because there are about forty people on their way up here right now." He wasn't kidding. Within minutes, our room was crawling with cowboys. We kept saying, "No party here! We don't even have alcohol." They quickly exhausted the little that we did have, and they told us to follow them. I had no idea where we were going, but we followed the drunken crowd into the elevators. It was one of the funniest moments of my life. We all piled into an elevator laughing and talking. The doors opened to the lobby and two security guards stood directly in front of the elevator. There was dead silence—until one guy near the front of the elevator said, "Oh sorry. We must be lost. We were looking for our room and this isn't it!" The doors closed again and everybody erupted into laughter. We then went up to the fifth floor. I didn't know whose room we were going to, but it was at the end of the hall and the double doors indicated that it was a suite. When the door opened, I was shocked to see the CEO standing there. Everyone walked right into his room and resumed the party. It really was funny. He seemed shocked, but made no attempt to stop it. That night, Christine hooked up with a very famous cowboy and I was jealous. Shelly met a man the night before, and I was on my own. That didn't stop me from attending many more events.

I had my share of indiscretions, but the purpose of this book is not to share every detail of my sex life, but to examine who I was, how I reacted to what happened to me, and how I have grown since then.

chapter 24

My New Life

I turned to the fire department to fill a lot of my spare time. When I wasn't at work, I was responding to rescue calls. I also decided to become a firefighter—not because I had a lifelong desire, but because it was badass and I wanted to prove to myself that I *could!* I made it through Firefighter I and II, along with some other specialized training. I was now the only female firefighter in the department, and I was assigned to the "attack squad" after my probationary rotations. Everyone wanted to be on the attack truck, as it was always the first truck out the door and its crew members were considered the "cowboys" of firefighters. It was unheard of for a female to be assigned to that squad. In fact, one of the captains had been heard saying there would never be a female on that squad as long as he was on it. I guess he changed his mind.

My job at American Express also was going very well! I'd been there only a few years and already won every award the company offered for my level of employment. My salary almost doubled and I completed a course for high-performing employees to train for management positions. My class was the first of this type. We traveled to Minneapolis once a month and learned many aspects of employee management. I was lucky that my boss, JoAnne, was a mentor in the class, and two other women from my region were in the class. I always had traveling companions. JoAnne's boss, Lydia, also supported me every step of the way! When it was announced that the office I worked in was closing, I returned to the main call center as an agent on a different set of accounts. I was versatile as I knew all three airline computer systems. If the accounts I was normally assigned to were slow and the larger account was busy, I would simply move to another desk and work on them.

One day I approached Lydia and expressed my frustration. I was ready for a promotion, but I didn't see opportunity for upward movement any time soon. Lydia told me she had business that wanted to move to Milwaukee, but she was not able to hire enough agents to handle it. If I could provide the solution to hiring more agents, there would be the potential need for another team leader. I told her about something that I had read in a company newsletter—the Travel Education Program (TEP), which had been successful in other cities. TEP taught applicants from other customer service positions about the travel business. I was astonished when she said, "Okay. It's your project. Take it and run."

This worker bee was now in charge of running a revolutionary new program in Milwaukee! I was amazed that I had been entrusted with such a huge, and *expensive*, undertaking.

When the program was completed, additional business from the Michigan call center would be relocated to Milwaukee. The client business was managed as two separate companies, but they had merged and the travel program was being streamlined. The TEP program was a moderate success. Four possible agents were identified when it finished. One had dropped out early in the program. Of the remaining five, one flunked out, three were promoted as travel counselors, and one was promoted as a travel support counselor. Some additional counselors were hired and I finally got my promotion as team leader.

I managed a team with a partner named Craig. He and I had worked together years earlier for another agency. In fact, he was the first person I reached out to when I returned to the travel industry, and he directed me to Lydia. We got along very well and, when it was determined that the team was now too large for just one leader, I took the promotion to be Craig's equal. A supervisory agent named Gloria worked under us to run the International/VIP team. The three of us could not have gotten along better. Each agent reported to only one of us, but they never knew which one. (The only exception was Gloria's team. Her charges reported to her to solve problems, only escalating to Craig or me as needed.) Craig,

Gloria and I discussed how we wanted to manage as a team. We divided up the normal tasks of leaders according to what we most liked or what our strengths were. We had the most fabulous boss in the world in Lydia. She had been our boss at the previous agency. She was a big believer in professional development and empowerment. She let us find our way and was very pleased with how it worked.

Craig and I decided early on to present a united front to our employees at all times. We covered all scenarios and functioned almost as one person. Historically, Craig's team turned in stellar results, so I wasn't worried about the "numbers" side of the business that first year. Unfortunately, with the expanded team, the numbers weren't remarkable. In fact, they could not have been worse, according to company standards. It was time for me to learn about numbers—and did I ever! I took a weeklong class in Phoenix and made a lot of important contacts there. I worked with Lydia to get a better understanding of our reporting systems. I also reached out to my former mentor from the Management Training Program, who was now the Regional Financial Manager.

Craig and I turned that team completely around by the end of the second year. Craig received almost all of the credit for employee satisfaction; the employees never really knew what I was working on. That's because I was now the "numbers person." Each month, Craig and I met with each employee to discuss performance. We extrapolated how current performance would be rated if it continued for the remainder of the year. We broke down the results to the hour. For example, taking just one more call per hour might help an employee reach the next highest rating. When explained in those terms, agents understood their jobs better and they began to create higher goals for themselves. (I came up with a way to pull data from numerous reporting systems to calculate those numbers, Gloria created a form to allow us to do the calculations automatically as the numbers were plugged in, and Craig and I delivered them together.)

Lydia also allowed us leeway in how we provided incentive for the team to reach specific monthly goals. For example, if the team exceeded a specific number of transactions in a given month, Craig, Gloria, and I cooked lunch for the agents in the breakroom as a reward. The three of us often met in the "Huddle Room" and bounced ideas off one another. I was sure the employees thought all we ever did was goof around in there, because some of our ideas were so "off-the-wall" that we would just burst into laughter. But, in the end, the crazy ideas often turned out best. Both Craig and Gloria called me "the ideas person."

I followed the team's finances *very* closely all year. By year-end, by all accounts we expected to achieve the highest possible rating. When the final results arrived, a single $50 charge on the report dropped us to the second-best level. I called the finance manager and went around with her on the issue, but there was no changing it. I went to Lydia to express my frustration over this late charge, and it was the one and only time I ever saw her snap. Ratings for each office ran from 1 being the best to 5 being the worst. She said to me, "Every other office in the region is either a 4 or 5, so I'm sorry, but I have no sympathy for you getting a 2 instead of a 1!" And with that, we missed our goal by $50. The team was disappointed, as all of us were. Our annual raises were all based on performance. But we still transformed from being the worst-performing office in the region to the best in just one year. That year, I won the Trendsetter award, given to the top 7 percent of employees. My goal was the Pacesetter award for the top 5 percent, but that would have meant taking Pacesetter away from one of the agents who really deserved it, so I didn't mind. I already had a Pacesetter award on my résumé.

And then, we all experienced the day that would change the world: September 11, 2001. I was at the office and a meeting planner stood up and said, "My caller just told me that a plane has hit the World Trade Center." I turned on the TV in the break room just in time to see the second plane hit the towers. I immediately went to my desk and called the Red Cross, knowing they would need more firefighters in New York City in the days to come. I warned my boss that my leaving to help was a possibility, but the Red Cross never called back.

As it turned out, that was a good thing. While I loved my job and had become very good at it, I never thought of what we did as "important." All of my "off time," as well as my previous jobs, were spent in the world of life and death. I had never realized that my role as a leader of the team was so important. It suddenly occurred to me that I was responsible for the safety, well-being, and resources of everyone in that call center, and that they were responsible for reassuring all of our travelers and helping them get home to their families. Fortunately, I learned to run new reports that identified where all of our clients were at any given time. I must have been one of the first to think of this, because I was able to get into the system. Craig, Christine and I were able to confirm quickly that we had no clients on the hijacked planes. Our biggest, immediate challenge was to get the others home to their families. I was on hourly conference calls with upper management to discuss business continuation plans, and then I shared that information with the team. Craig and I were kept moving throughout the next couple of weeks. Christine was busy keeping the client travel manager "in the loop," advising him where each traveler was and what our plan was to get him/her home. I was so proud to see our team thinking "outside the box" by planning rental car routes. The team identified clients who had rental cars (they were all rented within hours) and located other employees of the client company on their way home. They had independently started planning "carpools" home. They also thought to start renting trucks from U-Haul and Budget when no cars were available.

chapter 25

Just Like Riding a Bike

I worked hard at the gym and lost a ton of weight. Firefighter class
certainly helped. I sought outdoor activities that I enjoyed to keep my
figure shrinking. Christine rode in a hard-core bike ride —150 miles over
two days—the previous year in support of the Leukemia and Lymphoma
Society. This year I wanted to join her, so I went out and bought a road
bike. I'd been doing spin classes at the gym, so how much harder could it
be to ride a real bike? I'm afraid that answer was *a lot!* The year I bought
the bike, Christine and I went out riding and found a trail that was not
yet paved. The gravel was packed. I did fine until I got too close to the
edge. The gravel took my front tire, the bike stopped and I flew over the
handlebars, landing on the gravel. I hurt a rib, but not badly. My wrist also
hurt, but I was more worried about my bike. (Road bikes are not cheap
and I didn't know the first thing about caring for mine.) We rode back to
the bike shop, got my bike checked out, and then we continued riding.
We rode another 18 miles. When I got home, my ribs were still a little
sore, but I didn't think too much about it. The next morning, I went to
the doctor. I got a splint for my wrist and an X-ray of my ribs, which hurt
so badly that I cannot even describe the pain. I ended up in bed for almost
six weeks with a fractured rib. Eventually I was sent to pain management
for a neuropathy of my ribs. (I always thought of pain management as the
doctor's version of, "I don't think there's a damned thing wrong with her,
but the pain doc will make her feel like I did something.") I didn't make
that charity ride that summer. Christine did and had a great time. I missed

a lot of fun that summer. I had so many new friends and we had made plans to go to concerts and festivals. Instead, I barely moved. Christine stopped by to bring me dinner most nights.

In the summer of 2003, I was *determined* to make it to the charity ride—and finish it. Christine didn't that year, because she was recovering from surgery. I did the training and was psyched for the morning of the ride. Christine was volunteering for the event, so she took my bike and me to the departure point, where I immediately made some new friends. Early on, we maintained a pace of about 17 mph, which was good for me; it didn't feel hard to keep up. After about 17 miles, we came upon a huge hill. Climbing was my weakness, so I lost the guys with whom I'd been riding. Halfway up the hill, I actually got off the bike and walked for a spell. Once over the hill, we enjoyed a long, but not-too-steep, descent. I rode down and thought, "Wow! 24 mph. That's *really* good for me!" I saw the first rest stop up ahead of us. I almost completed the first 20 miles! Then, without warning, my front tire got caught on a slight height difference between the road and the shoulder. And, at my descending speed, the bike stopped. My body continued to travel at 24 mph, and it came to a thud about 50 feet from my bike. At first, I just lay in the road trying to assess the damage. My entire left arm was road rash. I thought to myself, "The next 130 miles are going to suck." Then I tried to sit up. My right arm didn't want to get up with me. I knew it was *very* broken; I could feel the bones moving inside. The pain was unreal. As an EMT, I was trained to assess the entire patient, despite what the person complains of, because major pain can mask other injuries. I now understood that as I looked at my left shoulder and arm and thought "Wow! That looks like it should really hurt, but I can't feel it." An ambulance was called. I knew most of the EMTs in the county because I'd been one for about seven years, but I didn't know the ones who arrived to treat me. The person who assessed my injuries should never have passed EMT school! First of all, the mechanism of injury should have told them to put me on a long board with a neck brace, in case I had injured my spinal cord. Even worse for me, the EMT who tried to splint my arm did not know how to use their new "vacuum splints." No matter how many times I told him that the arm was not stabilized, because the bones were still moving, he couldn't manage to fix it. Finally, I just said, "Forget it!

I'll just hold it together!" And so I rode to the hospital holding my arm together, hoping they would put a cast on it so I could catch the bike ride at the overnight spot. No such luck. I had to wait a *long* time in the E.R. for the orthopedic surgeon to arrive, and then the doc only confirmed what was already known from the X-ray. Surgery was needed. The pain was so unreal that the morphine didn't help. The only drug that *did* work was Demerol, but it made me vomit violently as soon as they gave it to me. We developed a system in which the nurse (whom I'd long known as one of the kindest nurses in the county) handed me the puke bucket and shot me up with the Demerol. Whatever worked.

The surgeon deemed that surgery could wait until Monday. Massively large splints and bandaging were placed on my arm and I was sent home for the weekend. By the time I got home, the pain in my left arm and wrist also became noticeable. I called the fire chief right away, because I was scheduled in a few weeks to sing the National Anthem at a truck "wet down" ceremony for a neighboring fire department. I also notified the captain of my own squad to tell him that I would be out of action for a while, because I broke my right arm and possibly the left wrist. (The surgeon said he'd look at the wrist on Monday while I was under anesthesia.) The captain picked up the phone just as I was leaving a message on his machine. He practically yelled, *"You broke both of your arms?"* I explained that we still weren't sure the left was broken. I had to admit, it was kind of funny. Needless to say, I wouldn't be on my bike again anytime soon. Over the next few years, the guys in the firehouse cracked jokes about getting me a tricycle or having me ride in a bubble.

Christine pulled out the sleeper sofa in my apartment that first night, and I said, "What are you doing?" She replied, "Getting ready for bed." I said, "You don't have to stay. I'm sure I'll be fine." I couldn't have been more wrong. She settled me into my bed, and after she left, I couldn't even pull up my own covers. I called her in to do that and to give me pain pills.

The next few weeks were one hell of a challenge for both Christine and me. My parents went up north on vacation right after my injury. Christine spent the entire first week with me. She took me to the hospital for the surgery on Monday and then spent the next week waiting on me hand and foot. She developed a system for icing my arms. She bought big bags of ice and kept them in a cooler. She double bagged each ice pack and placed one on each arm, wrapping them in place with a pillowcase. She bought me groceries that I could easily pick up and eat, since I had no use of my right arm and limited use of my left.

My parents returned to town after a week, and Christine had a date. Mom and Dad came up to take care of me. In the few hours they were there, they understood what Christine had been dealing with for over a week. They were more than happy when she came back. I kept saying, "No. Christine does it like this." After the first week, Christine was back to work and no longer slept in my apartment. She put my pain pills in a bowl covered by a saucer and left a glass of water on my nightstand. That way, I could wake up and take my pills without having to open anything—and without fear that my cats may get into my pills. She stocked me up with chicken nuggets and hot dogs so I didn't have to open cans or jars. I just popped them in the oven. The absolute *worst* experience was that Christine had to help me shower. I couldn't use my arms to wash myself. My right arm still had a massive incision that had to remain covered, and my left arm was not much help. Imagine being a full-grown adult and having to have your friend give you a shower.

chapter 26

Dream Job Turned Nightmare

I returned to work after about six weeks, only to hear the announcement that our client (that currently employed me, my partner Craig, and about 30 travel counselors), pulled its business due to outside circumstances. We were informed that American Express planned to add new business in our center, because we were the top-performing office in the country, in terms of cost per transaction. In the meantime, some travel counselors would be laid off, while others would be offered temporary assignments in other locations. The decisions were to be based on seniority and performance. A number of us were assigned to a beta testing project in Phoenix.

The new job was quite boring. We made reservations on a new computer-booking platform that the company had been developing for some time. I was shocked to see how far they were from completion. Our job was to make reservations on the computer and see whether the transactions worked or failed. I was the quality reporting person. When a reservation failed, I would see if I could repeat the failure. If yes, I would send it to the programmers. If not, I would send it through. We worked from 8:00 a.m. to 4:30 p.m., and we stayed at a luxury resort. Most weeks, we flew out on Monday morning and flew back on Friday afternoon. I got tired of flying back and forth for no reason, so I began staying in Phoenix for two weeks at a time. Why not enjoy the luxury resort and meals on the company without the hustle and bustle of airports and chaos?

The one issue that kept coming up while in Phoenix was my arm. The incision had not yet healed and I still wore a splint. I called my doctor from Phoenix on more than one occasion, and I visited a walk-in clinic to be seen. It turned out I was allergic to the dissolvable stitches the doctor had used, and my body tried to reject them rather than heal. I was anxious to get home to dinner each day so that I could take my pain pills and, sometimes, cut out a stitch or two. I still had considerable pain, despite the fact that the doctor told me I should feel fine. It would be a long time before I felt "fine" again.

Craig and I were assigned to Phoenix, along with about five other agents. Since we were the only two with company credit cards, one of us had to go to dinner with the others every night. We allowed ourselves one day a week to stay in our own room to order room service while the other took charge of "dinner duty."

About six weeks into the Phoenix assignment, I got a call from Lydia, who was now our director. She said a client wanted to move its business to Milwaukee. I now had to pack up and change from a summer wardrobe to a winter one, as I was Boston bound. Craig and I were to fly to New York to meet the client. We planned to wear our best power suits, but Craig had just lost a lot of weight and didn't have one that fit. He was about the same size as my dad, so I took him over to my parent's house and got Craig decked out for the trip. The day was to be quick—in and out. Lydia flew with us, and a town car picked us up at the airport. We went to the office, talked with the client, and then we headed back to the airport. Lydia was known to be very frugal, so when she took us to the airline club instead of a restaurant, we both thought we were not getting a meal before flying home. Craig and I were both starving, so we tried to fill up on the complimentary cheese and crackers in the club. We must have looked like a couple of freaks who hadn't eaten in a year. It was quite funny! Each of us had a pile of empty wrappers from single-serve cheese and crackers sitting in front of us. Then, when it was time to leave the club and head towards our gate, Lydia asked, "Do you want to stop for a bite to eat?" I am most certain that the look on our faces was priceless! We looked at each other and could not stop giggling.

The following week, Craig was sent back to Phoenix while I was sent to Boston to work in the office of the client that would be moving to Milwaukee. I felt like such a traitor, because I worked side by side with people there, knowing they were about to lose their jobs so that my team could stay employed. I met our new office manager, Rainy, who planned to move to Milwaukee with the account.

A downside of traveling to Boston was that renting a car was not recommended. I took taxicabs everywhere I needed to go, which meant I had to pay cash and expense it later rather than using my corporate credit card. Fortunately, my hotel was very nice and right across the street from the famous Faneuil Hall Marketplace. I found plenty of places to eat and shop. Unfortunately, I missed Phoenix and being with my co-workers. Boston was lonely. I was ready to get off the road.

Eventually, the announcement was made official and Craig and I returned to Milwaukee and began a hiring frenzy. Rainy also moved to Milwaukee about this time. She immediately struck me as a two-faced know-it-all who needed to feel important, but I tried to give her the benefit of the doubt. She seemed to mention her MBA in every sentence. Newsflash: having a degree does not mean you're smart!

I had the comfort of knowing that my former boss, Lydia, was now her boss, so I knew everything would still be done with integrity.

During the past two or three years, Craig and I proved we could be successful in managing as a team. We were used as mentors for other Leadership Teams across the country. In fact, we were mentoring a pair of Team Leaders who worked under Rainy at the time. I had also been sent to Chicago for a few weeks to mentor a Team Leader there who was having difficulty. Our record spoke for itself.

One special gift Craig had given to me while working together was an introduction to the work of Dr. Wayne Dyer. Craig had undergone a personal transformation and had become very positive and spiritual. There was a new "peace" about him. We talked a lot about it, and one day he brought a book for me to read. It was entitled *You'll See it When You Believe it*, by Dr. Dyer. Once I read my first Wayne Dyer book, I couldn't get more of them quickly enough. Craig and I talked about how amazing it would be to actually see Dr. Dyer speak in person.

Upon moving to Milwaukee, I'm certain Rainy was intimidated by the fact that Craig and I had a solid working relationship with each other, and with her boss. Many members of the team had been working under us for four years now. Rainy had a strong need to be in control. She immediately tried to change our management style by separating our teams. She wanted each of us to be responsible *only* for those who directly reported to us. She didn't push us too hard on this, because her boss created our team's management and was in the next office over. Rainy, however, consistently undermined our authority when she encouraged agents to come directly to her with questions. During the first couple of weeks, it created no problems as I was completely overwhelmed by the demands of the client. Hourly emails with call statistics and reports were expected. The client requested constant communication with either Craig or me. In my opinion, those roles should have been reversed, because Rainy already had a relationship with the client and was responsible for the overall account. Craig and I managed the daily operations of the team. Rainy laughed a lot and was very bubbly, but I saw through her right from the start. I took comfort in knowing that Lydia was still her boss. Sometimes, when Rainy suggested something that went completely against our code of ethics or how we had been successful in the past, I said to her, "Have you talked to your boss about this?" If she asked why, I told her whatever story had me convinced that Lydia would *not* want things done that way.

After one month of working with this new client, our call statistics were dismal, to say the least. Between the intricacies of the client's travel policy, introducing many new agents to the account, breaking in a new computer system, and the new booking platform that was finally rolled out for beta testing, it took much more time to make each reservation. As a result, calls were not being answered as quickly as expected; sometimes callers were kept on hold for a very long time. One particular day, the call statistics were very bad. I was in charge of sending statistics three times a day to the client's travel manager. When Rainy came out of her office and saw what the stats were, she told me to "fudge the numbers" and lie to the client in my next report. I told her I was not comfortable with that and, if she wanted to do that, than she should send the report herself.

It bothered me for a few days. Finally, I went to Lydia and told her what had happened. I was never asked to fudge numbers again. However, things in the company began to change rapidly. Layoffs were occurring across the country as small to mid-sized call centers were being consolidated into "mega centers." Our director, Lydia was among the first to go. Christine also was gone. Without Lydia in the lead, Rainy was free to do as she pleased. What she pleased was always unethical, immoral, or a plain old power trip. She set out to break up our team, piece by piece. Luckily, Craig and I were solid in our history and continued to shield the team from most of her irrational orders. Because she was so bubbly and always joking with the employees, they were never shown what she was really like.

Something great happened about this time: Craig and I discovered that Dr. Wayne Dyer was going to be a keynote speaker at Celebrate Your Life, a holistic conference that takes place in Phoenix. The conference was to be packed with motivational authors and speakers. We somehow convinced Rainy that this would be an excellent opportunity for us all to learn, grow, recharge our batteries, and acquire new skills. She agreed! Before long, we were booked for the conference in Phoenix. Rainy was supposed to attend with us, but she came up with a last-minute excuse and did not show up. Craig and one of our other colleagues joined me. That weekend opened my eyes to a whole new world of opportunities! I couldn't put down the books written by authors who were at the show! One of the authors I resonated with was Alan Cohen. I've probably read every book he's ever written. Celebrate Your Life set the foundation for me. I now believed, without a doubt, that we have the ability to create the world around us through our thoughts, beliefs, and intentions. My certainty of this came in handy many times down the road.

Every year, the client held an annual meeting for all the travel suppliers. That year, it was to be in San Francisco. Rainy asked Craig, Gloria, and me to volunteer to plan all of the flights and airport transfers. I told her I would do it, but I also reminded her that I was taking a family medical leave to have surgery on both of my wrists just before the trip. Any last-minute changes had to be handled by someone else. As it turned out, I turned it over to one of our VIP counselors who had held my current job when I'd been hired. He put *a lot* of work into it, as airport transfers were significant and had been started by the time I had my first surgery.

Not long after that trip, Rainy was let go. The manager from the smaller accounts office next door assumed the task of overseeing both offices. I had known that manager for years and hadn't heard one good thing about her management style. I was pleasantly surprised at how smart she was and how quickly she picked up the account and our financials. Her work skills were incredible; she just didn't have solid people skills. As for me, I saw the writing on the wall and started looking for employment elsewhere. People continued to be released as the company downsized. I was supposed to be "towing the company line" by reassuring our agents that our office would not be closing, but I *knew* it wouldn't be long. Ironically, when Christine was let go from her jobs as account manager and meeting planner, Craig and I hired her as a VIP counselor. It didn't pay nearly what she had been making but it was something until she found another job. She eventually found a job as an office manager at a Jewish preschool. After about eight months or so, Christine was hired back by American Express as an account manager in the Meeting Planning Division. She was very good at her job. When she vacated her job at the preschool, she recommended me for the job and set up the interview.

She warned me that I needed a skirt for the interview, because this was a very strict branch of the Jewish faith; women were not to wear pants. The salary was significantly more than what Christine had made there, but she sold them on the idea that if they wanted a quality employee, they had to pay the market price.

The day arrived when I was given my annual evaluation at American Express. Although Rainy was no longer in Wisconsin, she was present by phone to deliver the evaluation while my new boss, Bonnie, sat in. Craig and I spent the last year building a team from scratch—bonding them together, empowering them to create and sign our office laws and guidelines—while we pacified a *very* demanding client, traveled frequently, and worked four 12-hour shifts each week. (Craig and I always tried to work four 10-hour weeks to ensure we didn't top 50 hours a week; it was easier to not come in than to leave on time.) Rainy agreed to our schedules or we wouldn't have worked them. I knew that during the past year I had worked harder than in any other year. I also knew that, since our results weren't good, I couldn't expect the high marks—1s and 2s—that I usually got on my performance appraisal. Although Rainy did not like me personally, I expected her to stay professional when it came to ratings. She did not. My appraisal was almost all 4s! She was very careful not put things into writing that she knew were illegal or immoral. But she did speak them. She mentioned that I had dumped work on the VIP counselor just before leaving for the big trip, despite my early warning that I would be out on medical leave. Rainy said Craig and I did whatever we wanted despite her orders. When I asked her for an example, she cited up our work schedules. I pointed out that she never expressed to us that she did not want us working four 10-hour shifts or we wouldn't have done it. I pointed out that using FMLA against me was against federal labor laws. Rainy brought up so many nitpicky things that it was clear this was personal. I tried to argue, but it was no use. She was crafty enough to use only company approved lingo in writing. When she hung up the phone, I stayed in Bonnie's office for a few minutes while crying. I said it would have been better if Rainy had simply said, "Due to the office results, I had to give one of the leaders a 4, and I picked you." When I left Bonnie's office, still crying, Craig and I met in the "Huddle Room." I told him what happened, and he could not believe it. He received a much better rating than I did, even though he said I had done the majority of the heavy lifting. I was devastated! I had never been judged below average on any employee evaluation in my entire career!

chapter 27

Saved by the Bell

That very afternoon I got a call from the director of the preschool, offering me the job of office manager. It paid more than I was currently making, but I was certain to lose any difference in lost benefits. I wanted to get out of my job, and get out now, so I accepted the preschool position on the spot. I already wrote my letter of resignation and delivered it to Bonnie's office. She looked resigned, more than anything else. I think she knew deep down that I was a great employee—and our roles easily could have been reversed if she hadn't beaten me out for a team leader job just before I'd gotten this one. (My prediction that the American Express office would close was confirmed just two weeks after I left.)

I started work at the preschool exactly two weeks later. Actually, I went in earlier, on my off days during those two weeks, to work with Christine. She was there for one more week after I started, so she did her best to train me quickly. I had a *lot* to learn, and it was very overwhelming at first. I was stuffed into a tiny office behind the kitchen. I shared it with a part-time bookkeeper, fundraiser, and Jewish coordinator. They had varied schedules and shared the one desk. My office and computer were always crowded. If I stepped out long enough to use the restroom, someone would be using my computer when I got back.

The first six months at the job were extremely difficult! I didn't understand the Jewish culture and wasn't familiar with its traditions and pronunciations. I wasn't familiar with the names. I had to ask every caller to spell his or her first name for me. I required direction from my boss on a lot of issues, and she was a *very* hard woman to catch! In addition to being the director at our preschool, she also was principal of the K-8 school, upstairs from the preschool. I *still* struggled with my right arm.

Once I started to get a feel for the place, I began doing things without waiting on direction from my boss. I left her letters and notes on her desk, and she would make notes or changes and leave them back on my desk. This system served us well, until we both got to know enough about each other that we no longer needed many revisions or rewrites. Thank goodness!

In time, I learned that my role was not simply to be an assistant, but to offer public relations to parents, serve as medical technician as needed, be a sounding board for teachers, and be responsible for the daily running of the school. I learned the timeframes for fall registration, summer camp registrations, and family events. I created the school calendar each year and used it as my guide to know when to begin working on events long before they came up. That first year was very difficult, because I was expected to know how to respond to particular events and Jewish holidays, and I had no idea.

I learned about the different types of kosher food. Although ordering food was not one of my responsibilities, I realized we were paying *far* too much for many of the items we bought regularly. The general belief was that these items, particularly dairy, could only be purchased from the one kosher service in town. I started asking the Jewish teachers where they bought their groceries and immediately arranged for a local store to order and deliver our 25 gallons of milk per week for $1.25 less per gallon. My boss began to trust me and appreciated my initiative. Although she was never one to give praise, her approval became more evident, as she allowed me to act independently. I learned so much about the Jewish culture and developed admiration for the traditions and dedication. I still went to my boss or another observant Jewish teacher when I had questions, when I was uncertain whether something was allowed and when I questioned whether something I said or did was appropriate. For example, every Friday the parents wished me a "Good Shabbos" or told me, "Shabbat shalom." I wanted to return the good wishes, but didn't know if I should because I was not of the Jewish faith. My boss appreciated that I was thoughtful enough to ask and assured me it was in no way offensive.

In my second year at the preschool, the building expanded significantly in size. At the end of the school year, we vacated the building to allow for construction to begin. The other two schools that used the building were not affected by the work, but our preschool ran a summer camp. We scrambled to rent space in a nearby school with indoor and outdoor facilities that were age appropriate for our children. Once the location was selected, we began the moving process. Every item in the school was tagged to move either to storage or to a classroom or office in the summer space. I arranged for the installation of a kosher stove in the kitchen, the computer network and phone lines and portable air conditioners. The offices were configured to meet our needs. It was truly an amazing trick when it all came together! It certainly earned the praise (which was *very* rare) and confidence of my boss.

My right wrist still was painful despite the best efforts of three surgeons. One day my boss said to me, "I can make a call if you want to get you in with Dr. Chamoy." I asked who that doctor was, and she explained that he was one of the leading hand surgeons in the country, and that he worked here in Milwaukee! I said, "Sure!" My first appointment with Dr. Chamoy was so different than it had been with any other hand surgeon. He actually sat and listened to the history of my injury and the attempts that had been made to repair it. It was as if I could see the wheels turning in his head. Every once in a while, he stopped my conversation and asked, "Where's the surgeon's report on that?"—among many other questions. By the time he was done listening, Dr. Chamoy already had a working theory about why my wrist was injured. He believed I had an entrapped nerve and some torn ligaments. He injected a numbing medicine to confirm his theory about the nerve, and then he sent me for an MRI to confirm the torn ligaments.

After the results of the MRI arrived, the doctor informed me that I had at least two torn ligaments, and he wouldn't know about the third until he got in there to look. Christine took me in to what she now referred to as "my hospital" on the day of the surgery. When I awoke in the recovery room, I was told that the damage was much worse than anticipated. One of the main ligaments in my wrist was almost completely severed. (I was *so* glad I didn't listen to all the people who had been telling me I should just "learn to live with it.") I needed a complete reconstruction of my wrist, and I would be in a cast for six months and unable to lift anything for a year. I said, "Well, why even wake me up? Let's go." Of course, it didn't work that way. A reconstruction has to be scheduled in advance. I went back to work for a short time and then went back to the hospital for the reconstruction. During the surgery, temporary pins were placed in my wrist to hold everything together. The larger bone in my forearm was shortened so it was the same size as the other bone, and that required another plate and screws. My wrist was then placed in a cast. Within a few days, I knew the cast wasn't going to work. Somehow, the cast pushed on the pins, the pins hit a nerve, and I screamed out in pain! The doctor replaced what had been done with a half cast, which worked much better! I worked as much as I could, and I was frustrated at not being able to type as quickly as usual. But my management skills were more important to the running of summer camp than my typing skills. My boss was incredibly patient and understanding during this time.

I took an anti-depressant called Wellbutrin for a number of years. I originally was prescribed the drug to help me quit smoking. Whenever I went to my doctor and complained about fatigue, he diagnosed depression and encouraged me to use anti-depressants. I didn't *feel* depressed at that time, but the Wellbutrin helped me lose weight and gave me more energy. I also asked my doctor to screen me for rheumatoid arthritis, the only disease I was aware of that could explain why my body always hurt. He assured me I did *not* have it, but he ran the test anyway. When the test came back negative, he sent me a little "I told you so" note, along with the results. He never dug any further to find out what was truly wrong with me. I was led to believe that the pain and fatigue were "all in my head," so I just kept pushing forward.

That summer, I was asked to work with the board on the preschool's annual fundraiser. I thought it sounded like great fun, but it seemed they were starting awfully early. The fundraiser took place in winter. Once I committed to the project, I found out just how wrong I was. There was so much to be done! The board members wanted to play a big role in selecting the venue, and there was not much agreement among them. The date of the event also was an issue. We were not allowed to do fundraising during certain times of the year, due to some restrictions by the Jewish Parent Organization, which donated money to the school. We also were restricted during that time from seeking out sponsors and donors. Sponsors were key to profitability. We also had to design, print and mail out "save the date" cards, invitations and an event booklet. I worked extensively on the mailing list, which needed a major overhaul! I also helped the designers on the printed materials and banners. I solicited auction items, ran the annual raffle ticket sales, and pulled together all of the donations that had been either solicited or donated by the board members. I needed to hire a caterer to prepare kosher appetizers without using the ovens in the venue, unless a rabbi first koshered them—and that was essentially impossible within our working parameters. We also had to plan for decorations, plates, glasses, plastic utensils, storage for auction items and much more. The first year I was there, the fundraising coordinator—who had since left and was not replaced—handled almost all of this. Prior to the auction, I worked many days from 6:00 a.m. to 10:00 p.m. I was so stressed and nervous by the time the big day arrived that I felt like I could drop. Overall, the event was a success. The "volunteers" I recruited to assist me were Christine, my former boss JoAnne, and my former colleague Gloria, who now worked as the executive administrative assistant at our Jewish parent organization. Despite a glitch with the check out database, these women all thought on their feet and kept the event afloat. I was extremely thankful for them as I was utterly exhausted by then!

Another life-altering event happened that summer, but I told no one. One night, Christine and I went out to a local bar. I sat at the bar nursing my first drink when a man who used to work there sat down next to me. He was clearly either very drunk or on some kind of drugs. He was creeping me out as he tried to make conversation, while leering at me. He offered me a cigarette. I said, "I would have to have had a whole lot more to drink than this to want a cigarette." About this time, I got my second drink. Not long thereafter, I began to feel "funny." I sensed danger from the man next to me, so I walked over to a table occupied by four large college students and planted myself next to the biggest one, whom I had been looking at earlier. This was my last clear memory. I remember that I got into the passenger seat of a car. I thought Christine was driving. I had only one snapshot of memory after that, of having sex with the large man in my bed. I heard him say this was great and that I'd better answer the phone when he called. When I woke in the morning, he was gone. I was in some pain, and I discovered at least three used extra-large condoms in my bedroom. I didn't report it immediately, because I felt stupid and embarrassed. I didn't believe the large guy had anything to do with me being drugged. He probably thought I was an eager and willing participant. Date rape drugs do that to women. They make them lose their inhibitions and do things they would not normally do. (And let's face it: I'd done this many times before of my own free will.) Date rape drugs also block memory. Christine was the only person who knew what happened that night, and I kept it that way for about a year. I told myself it wasn't as if I'd never brought men home before. In fact, I've shared only the most important stories in this book. This book was never to be about my sexual escapades, but about how I spent many years not respecting myself at all. I cannot even think about how many men I'd slept with from age 18 to 38. This is not something I am proud of. It is something I hope you will learn from.

Back at the preschool, I built many great relationships with the parents, teachers, children—and even my boss in her *very* understated way. One day, she brought in a consultant to study time management with key personnel in both schools. For two weeks, I logged what I was doing for practically every minute of the day. Then the consultant interviewed me. My boss never told me the results of this study. However, the vice principal of the school upstairs was in the meeting when the results were delivered. She told me that the consultant began the presentation by noting, "First of all, Bridgette does far too much. There is no way one person could do everything she does and do it well." My boss never shared this with me, but it somehow made me feel better—until she began hiring additional help. She brought in a receptionist, an assistant director, a fundraiser, and a new business manager. I wondered what exactly was left for me to do. The answer was: the annual fundraiser—my least favorite thing to do!

Many good things came out of that job for me. One was meeting a woman named Betty, who had three children. She was a registered dietician, but I didn't know that until she donated some of her time as an auction item. I hired her to be my personal dietician, and I began to lose weight on a weekly basis. I also joined some other members of the fire department in a 12-week boot camp at the local gym. We met twice a week and were put through the paces by one of the gym's toughest trainers. Eating better and working out more allowed me to drop from a size 18 or 20 down to a size 10! I was feeling great about myself! My weight went up and down throughout the years. I often used it as a protective shield to avoid attracting the attention of men. That way, I would not be raped again and I would not disrespect myself by sleeping with someone.

The recent weight loss was fabulous and I was *very much* looking forward to my annual cruise. For the past four years or so, my brother Ryan and I were roommates on a cruise every February with our brother John and his wife Sandy, along with many other friends and family. With my newfound looks and improved self-esteem, I was sure to have a great time!

chapter 28

Making Money Doing What I Love

I struggled financially and felt underappreciated in my role at the preschool. I liked it better when I had too much to do. Now, I delegated most of my responsibilities to the four people who had been hired since the time management study. I had been an EMT for more than fifteen years by then, and a firefighter for about seven. I loved being part of Emergency Medical Services. One day, on the way back from an ambulance call, the driver mentioned that the county had posted openings for two dispatchers. I didn't think dispatchers made enough money to live on, but when I looked it up, any pay cut would be offset by an improved benefit package. I turned in my application and was invited to test for the position, along with 125 other people. I was so shocked when I arrived for the test! The room was filled beyond capacity. Also testing was the father of a child who attended the preschool. He promised not to mention that he saw me. The test was harder than I expected, and I was certain that I did not stand much chance of being called back. I was called back within just a few days! I went to the sheriff's department for an interview and to take a typing test. I was thrilled that I'd made it that far, thinking they couldn't have called back too many people. Within days of my interview, Dispatch Supervisor Heidi called and advised me that I was among the top four candidates. At this stage, they wanted to be sure I was serious about the job, because they were about to refer me to the Detective Bureau. A detective would look into every aspect of my life and talk to friends, family and neighbors, along with all past and current employers. I was nervous about this, because only two spots were open, and I knew my boss would be upset once she knew I was looking for work. I finally decided to go for it. I was called in on a Saturday for an interview, which took a *very* long time. The detective asked me about all of the answers I had given on my 12-page background form. Then we spoke about my life. (Of course, we didn't cover my "secret life of shame.") During the next two weeks, the other candidates were interviewed. Every now and then, I heard from a friend or former employer that they had been interviewed about their interaction with me. After about two weeks, I received a phone call from the captain while I was at work. He asked me to come in for a meeting with the sheriff. I arranged to do so on my lunch hour that same day. I was so excited. I knew they would not be calling me in if they didn't have a job to offer! I accepted immediately. I advised them that I had already booked my non-refundable cruise for the upcoming February. I was so excited that I was actually going to make a living in emergency services. I was given the second shift on a rotating schedule, working from 4:00 p.m. to midnight, and most weekends. That didn't concern me, as I didn't go out much anyway.

When I started the job, the training was a bit harder than I thought. Dispatchers took a lot of things for granted that were difficult for a newcomer to understand. In addition, information in the training manual appeared far more complex than it actually was. I was a bit shocked at how low tech they really were! I swear, the dispatch center had to be the only room in the entire state that didn't have Caller ID! I started to create my own learning tools, and I ran them by Jack, the main training officer, to ensure my understanding was correct. He said no one had ever done that before. It seemed like common sense to simplify the more complex issues. I received glowing reviews throughout the twelve weeks of training.

Then, it was time for me to fly on my own. I was a bit nervous, because the technology in the dispatch center was *far* below the standards of what I expected. Rather than a policy and procedure manual, the staff issued memos and policies that were outdated and many of them superseded other memos. Each dispatcher interpreted every memo or policy differently. Reprimands could be issued at any time for interpreting a policy differently than it read—or if they just wanted to find something wrong.

I began that job on December 3, 2007. I was in peak physical condition and looked quite "hot" at the time, if I do say so myself. There was a lot of curiosity about me at work. Deputies were making comments behind my back. I heard a dispatcher from one of the local police departments on a recorded line tell one of our dispatchers that I was "hot." As a result, I was pretty leery of the guys who were particularly nice to me—ones who would call me from the car and ask if I wanted coffee or tea and then stop in the dispatch center to meet and/or talk with me.

chapter 29

Swept Off My Feet at Sea

In February 2008, I left for my annual cruise. We had a particularly large group going with us, including my next-door neighbors. I felt and looked great, and I expected a great experience. During the first night of the cruise, I stood at the craps table next to a man who had beautiful eyes. We didn't talk much, but he was gorgeous. The next evening was formal night. I felt absolutely amazing in my formal gown, with a fabulous hair-do, compliments of the ship's salon. I dropped by the casino and not much was happening yet. As I left the casino, I ran into the man with the beautiful eyes at the Champagne Bar. We began chatting and he bought me a drink. With a hopeful look in his eyes, he asked who was joining me on the cruise. When I told him that I was there with my brother, the relief was evident. From that moment on, we spent a lot of time together! He came to the show with me that night and met my family. During the show, he reached for my hand, and it was so comfortable! Later on that evening, he convinced me to meet him in the hot tub. I did. It took a while to get all of the pins out of my hair and change out of my gown (with Spanx, of course). I bought a new swimsuit just before the cruise, and it was very flattering. I wore a sheer black wrap as a skirt when I met him at the hot tub. It was so fascinating to watch him strip down to his swim trunks. I was relieved to see a little bit of flab on his tummy, so he wasn't physically perfect. As we sat in the hot tub, we began kissing and flirting, and cuddling. Then a woman joined us in the hot tub. She commented on what a beautiful couple we were, and then she asked how long we had been married. We laughed about that and explained that we had only met the night before. At one point, I left the hot tub to use the restroom. When I returned, six more people were in the hot tub. At first, I laughed to myself thinking, "This poor guy has been trying to get me alone, and now he doesn't stand a chance." After I got back into the hot tub, he introduced me to his friends and family. Some of them were beautiful people, some were kind of "gangster," and some were kind of trashy. They were *all* very nice to me. It was as if I was suddenly under the protection of the Mob. The man with the beautiful eyes was named Nathan. After our swim, we kissed goodnight and went back to our own cabins. (And let me tell you, that was *not* easy, but I was finally learning to respect myself. This seemed like a man with whom I wanted to be more than just a one-night stand.)

The following night, I came down with a cold. We spent the evening together, but I ended up getting seasick—or else I overdosed on cold medications. Either way, I ended up vomiting in a garbage can on an outer deck. I was so embarrassed and went back to my cabin to change. I returned to Nathan, and he was very sweet when I told him I needed to go back to my cabin and sleep, because I didn't feel well. I told him to go and spend time with his family. After I'd been asleep for a couple of hours, our cabin phone rang. One of Nathan's cousins was on the line. He said, "Bridgette, Nathan is standing outside your cabin door. Please go and let him in." I did. Nathan was clearly *very* drunk, and he crawled into bed with me. He said he'd wanted to be with me all night. It was very sweet. He didn't try anything. My brother was sleeping about four feet away. We held each other all night long and slept. In the morning, Nathan left to return to his own cabin. He asked me to join him there after I was up. I began to feel ill again as soon as I was headed that direction. I ended up vomiting in a garbage can on my way to his cabin. When he opened the door, I must have looked and smelled horrible. He was very sweet as he led me to his bed, had me lay down, and rubbed my back for a long while. Despite the fact that I told him to go out and have some fun, he stayed with me. He even went down to the café and brought me lunch. He reclined with me until I started to feel better.

By evening, I felt much better. I dressed in a short skirt, which showed off my super-strong legs, along with a sleeveless shirt. I felt sexy. I met

Nathan after dinner in the casino and we played craps and blackjack for a while. Honestly, all I thought about was getting back to his cabin. We left the casino early and went back to his cabin. He picked me up and wrapped my legs around him as he carried me to the bed. With the sparks that had been flying between us, even the simple act of undressing was incredibly sexy. We made love for the first time that night and I saw fireworks like I have never seen, before or since. It was the most beautiful experience, feeling him inside of me and looking into his beautiful and kind eyes. We spent the entire night making love over and over again. It was incredible. From that night on, I did not sleep in my own cabin. I loved the way he held me and put an arm around me whenever we were together. Typically, we didn't see each other until after dinner; then, we spent time playing craps in the casino. On the second formal night, I wore a very flattering gown. When Nathan's female cousins walked into the casino and saw me, they said, "Wow! You look sexy. Nathan is gonna be so happy!" He had a younger cousin who was 20. She was very funny. She said to me, "You have a great body for someone your age." I laughed and said, "Thanks. I work very hard at it." They asked how old I was. When I told them I was 36, they thought I was very old, but they went on to tell me what a wonderful man Nathan was and that he never just "hooked up" with women. They thought he must care a lot about me. I felt the same way about him. Despite our age difference—he was only 25—I felt comfortable and cherished with him. It was February 14, Valentine's day.

I felt like I'd been neglecting my own family and friends, because I spent every night with Nathan. I asked if he minded going to the nightclub and hanging out with my friends for a while. He didn't. We joined my group of friends for a bit. I felt a little awkward, knowing I was so much older than Nathan, and most of *my* friends and family were at least ten to fifteen years older than me. A slow song came on and Nathan and I strolled out to the dance floor. It was a magical moment for me. I was just thinking that it was the best Valentine's Day I'd ever had, when he said what I thought was "I love you." I really wasn't sure, so I asked him what he'd just said. Nathan replied, "Never mind." I floated on a cloud that entire week. One of the last nights before the end of the cruise, Nathan's brother (and cabin mate—we were plenty familiar by now) played at the final table for the ship's poker tournament. The winner received a free cruise to compete in the Royal Caribbean Tournament. As we watched the table, Nathan stood behind me with his hands in the front pockets of my skirt, while I leaned back on him. It was just a moment in time, but it was magic to me. Nathan's Mom asked me where he was, and I just tipped my head so she saw him behind me. I was sure she also noticed his hands in my pockets, but he didn't move. I felt like he was the most beautiful man I'd ever met, inside and out. (I guess I should have paid more attention to his brother, cousins, and friends. They were *not* all beautiful people. They got drunk and stupid a number of times throughout the cruise.)

On the last night of the cruise, I began crying while we were making love. He stopped and asked me why I was crying. I explained that what we had was really special and it was unlikely I would ever see him again. He was from Long Island and I lived in Wisconsin.

The cruise ended and I was sad to leave the ship. I was also still sick with my cold. The flight home was more than just depressing; it was a nightmare! Our flight from Miami to Chicago was canceled, and the airline tried to tell us we could not get home until the next Tuesday—three days away! I let my brothers talk to the airline representative, while I lay on my homemade bed in the aisle of seats near all of my friends. Ryan and I, along with another couple, ended up flying to St. Louis that night and then on to Milwaukee the following morning. Others in our group were routed all over the country so they could get home the following day, as well. I was miserable the whole time. Not only was I physically ill, I wished I was still in Nathan's arms. We fit so perfectly together.

chapter 30

Man of My Dreams Up in Smoke

Soon, I had to return to work, but I just wanted to be with Nathan. We began exchanging emails and phone calls, along with text messages, after we returned to our separate homes. I knew I had to see him again to see if our connection was something real. I arranged a couple of shift trades so that I could get a little extra time off to fly to New York in April. I was so excited and so nervous all at the same time!

Shortly before I was set to leave for New York, I went to the annual Fire Department Appreciation Night. It was good to see everyone and feel good about myself—and my physique. I had noticed throughout the night that one of the firefighters was flirting with me. No, flirting wasn't the right word. It was more like a primal, "I want you." I felt it with every fiber of my being. We were among the last to leave that night. He was maybe 22 years old. He walked me to my car, I said goodbye and after I got in, he leaned in and started kissing me. It got *really* hot, *really* fast! We were groping each other right there in the parking lot! I finally put a stop to it. He wanted to know why and I explained that I was going to New York the following week to see if what I'd found with Nathan was real. He reluctantly said, "Okay," and added that if it didn't work out with Nathan, then he and I *would* be sleeping together. In my confused state, my genius answer was, "Fine, but *just* sex. No dating!" I don't know what the hell I was thinking.

I only had a carry-on bag flying to New York, because I didn't want anything to delay being with Nathan. The 4-ounce liquid rule was recently instituted in airport security, so I ordered my hair products online and had them shipped directly to Nathan's address. I planned to pack them and check my bag on the flight home. As soon as I got to baggage claim, I saw Nathan standing there waiting for me. Everything else seemed to melt away! We kissed and just looked at each other for the longest time. I was lost in his eyes. After a long day and the flight, I was ready to eat. We decided to stop for a bite on the way home. At the restaurant, we sat across the table from each other holding hands and just looking into each other's eyes. The waitress made a number of comments about how in love we looked, how we couldn't possibly have seen the menu when we only had eyes for each other. We eventually looked at the menus and placed our orders. As we waited for our food, we continued holding hands and looking into one another's eyes—and we talked.

Once we finished eating, we headed for Nathan's home. Frankly, I just wanted to get to his apartment and rip his clothes off! During the drive, Nathan admitted to me that his apartment was above his parents, and that we had to go through their level to get to his. Translation: he lived with his parents! I was *so* not ready to face his parents. His family emigrated from Portugal, and they often spoke Portuguese in front of me, which made me feel uncomfortable. His mother spoke with a heavy accent and was quite imposing. Fortunately, it was quick and painless. Upstairs Nathan had his own living room, bedroom, bathroom, and what I would call an "almost kitchen"—a table, some shelves, and a refrigerator. We went right to bed! I was more than a little disturbed when, after we'd made love for a while, he left to go into the living room to smoke pot! He mentioned on the cruise that he and his friends sometimes smoked pot, but I understood that to be a rare party occasion. By morning, I realized that to Nathan, smoking pot was like drinking a cup of coffee. He did not do anything in between our lovemaking and smoking pot. Every time he got out of bed in the morning, he smoked pot.

This was a complete deal-breaker for me. I needed to get out and clear my head. While Nathan slept, I put on my running clothes and grabbed my iPod. He woke just as I was about to leave. He asked where I was going and I told him that I needed to go for a run. He told me about a track just a couple of blocks away and how to get there. On my way out, I ran into his mom in the kitchen. She was quite surprised that I was going running. As she looked me up and down, she asked if I went running every day. I said I tried to run more days than not. In truth, I always ran on a treadmill in the gym.

On my run, I thought, "What the hell do I do now? Here I was set to spend the next four or five days with the 'man of my dreams,' and he turned out to be a pot head." Around the first lap, Blake Shelton's song "Home" came on my iPod and I almost started to cry. I debated changing my flight and just going home, but that would cause a lot of drama and questions—not to mention that I wanted to be with Nathan. Despite the fact that I now knew a "relationship" could never be, I decided just to enjoy the days we had for now. I planned to drink in as much of him as possible before I said goodbye forever. I arrived on a Thursday night and planned to go home early on Tuesday, in time to go back to work. Nathan was scheduled to work on Sunday while I was there. It just so happened that one of the police officers, a reserve officer, and the dispatcher from the local police department who had said I was "hot," were in New York City that same weekend. We discovered that ahead of time and arranged to meet in Manhattan for lunch on Sunday. Nathan gave me directions to the nearest subway stop. It was only a few blocks away, but I still had to ask someone for help in locating it. I expected the train station to be larger than your average bus stop. Once I found the tiny little shelter, I bought my ticket to Penn Station and got on the next train. I texted the guys and told them I was on my way, and I asked where we were going to meet. It turned out they got on the wrong train and were going to be very late. That gave me time to walk from the station to the deli, rather than take a taxi. I enjoyed walking through Manhattan, confident and comfortable. (Although I confess, after about a mile, my favorite boots were no longer very comfortable.)

When I was close, I called to see where they were. They were almost there. Then, the biggest smartass of the three of them told me I had just walked right by them. For a brief moment, he had me questioning myself: "I know I haven't seen them much. I just hear their voices on a radio or phone. Is it possible that I walked by them?" Then I saw them up ahead.

It was nice to touch base with some friends from home and explain my situation—not that they could help, but it felt good to tell someone. It was a quick lunch and we said goodbye. I took a taxi back to Penn Station and returned about the same time Nathan got home from work.

While visiting Nathan in New York, we went to see a movie, which was great! We also visited his cousins at least twice. I didn't like going there. Nathan could see them any time, so shouldn't he want to spend what little time we had together with just me? When he and his cousins got together, they smoked pot. I didn't want to be around that at all, so I sat upstairs while they hung out downstairs. One night, we went to a surprise birthday party for one of his friends. I knew it would be difficult, because Nathan would be the only person I knew, and I didn't want to be clingy. I made up my mind to be social and meet new people. As a result, Nathan and I didn't spend a whole lot of time together at that party. I was relieved that some of his cousins and friends also were there, so ended up knowing a few people. The party wasn't nearly as bad as I expected.

During my last night in New York, we went out for a nice dinner; which I paid for! Really? You work full time, and live with your parents! I *flew* here to be with you, and you can't even spring for dinner? After dinner, Nathan wanted to go to his cousin's house again, this time for a poker game. I liked poker enough. I mean, he and I did meet in a casino! I thought I would enjoy that night, but I was wrong again. Shortly after we arrived, he and his cousin's husband grabbed the pipe and went down to the basement to smoke. I stayed upstairs, as I really did not approve at all. They were downstairs for more than an hour while I sat with his cousin in the living room watching a horrible reality show—and texting with Christine about the whole situation. Finally, Nathan remembered to come up and get me. (I suspected that it wasn't Nathan's idea to come upstairs, but that his cousin had texted him.) Nathan said they weren't smoking, but just hanging out. I finally went downstairs and did my best to remain oblivious to the large homemade bong on the floor and other drug paraphernalia around the room. Eventually, other family and friends whom I had met on the cruise arrived and we played poker. I tried to ignore the pipe being passed around. They all knew I worked in law enforcement and didn't approve. They didn't offer it to me; thank goodness for small favors. I didn't fare too well in the poker game, but I enjoyed the fun anyway.

The next morning, Nathan took me to the airport and we said our goodbyes. We kissed for a long time. I had tears in my eyes as I made my way through the airport. I knew I would never see this kind and beautiful man again (at least the man I had originally thought him to be). When I got home, everybody was eager to learn about my trip. I simply said it was fine, but that I knew there was to be no relationship. I told the real reason only to my closest friends. Shortly after that, I sent Nathan an email saying goodbye, as we both knew this could never work.

Truthfully, I was in a very weak state when I returned from New York. I just wanted to be held and cherished like that again. Despite my best intentions to break things off with Nathan, I continued to call and text him—and he did the same. In addition to Nathan, I had Jim to worry about. He was the young firefighter who wanted to sleep with me. It was a crazy time, as I was talking to both of them on the phone often—and essentially "sexting." By late May, I so badly wanted to be with Nathan again. Tickets from New York to Milwaukee were cheap. Nathan said he would come and see me on June 3. That was wonderful news. By having him come see me, I knew he could not use pot during the visit, because he couldn't get through the airport with it. I owned my own home and lived alone, so there would be no unwanted visitors or interruptions. I used my floating holiday at work so I could spend more time with him. Every time we talked, I asked if he bought his ticket yet. Then, instead of buying his ticket, Nathan just cut off all communication with me the week before he had planned to fly to Milwaukee. He stopped answering my calls, texts, and emails. Eventually, I became worried enough to call his home number. His mom said he was at work and asked, "Haven't you talked to him?"

I explained that Nathan had stopped talking to me, and that I was worried something had happened to him. As long as I knew he was okay, I could live with the "no longer speaking to me" part. It was hard, though. I never knew if he had finally opened his email or just decided this was for the best. I hated him for that. He never struck me as the chicken-shit type. He should have just come right out and told me himself. I was struck by the fact that I hadn't known this man's true character at all. However,

I still cherished memories of the time I was able to spend with the man I thought Nathan was. It was a magical experience for me. It gave me a little more clarity as to what I wanted in future relationships. I may have been a slow learner, but I was still learning—sometimes.

chapter 31

This is 911, and We Have an Emergency

I completed my training at the sheriff's department, and my probationary period was over. I was given a great review. It was so hard to keep my mouth shut, because I saw *so many* things that needed improvement—everything from a non-working TTY system (used by deaf people to make calls to each other, required by law) to a 911 mapping system that was accurate only 30 percent of the time to inconsistent reference sources, no policy and procedure manual, and so much more. Heidi, the dispatch supervisor, worked from 8:00 a.m. to 4:00 p.m. Monday through Friday. During that time, she rarely entered the Dispatch Center. There were no actual observations of the performance of the dispatchers other than what was told to her by other dispatchers or sergeants. Occasionally, she listened to recordings that were requested by other police or fire departments. She often left notes in our in-boxes with red writing that pointed out small spelling errors made on call records, restraining orders, or warrants; they were usually so trivial that it was laughable! In fact, when a new police department was added to our network, all of us made a mistake every once in a while. As soon as we recognized our error, we created a new call card, typed into the old one that it was a mistake and then canceled it. Despite the fact that we'd typed right into the call card that we'd made a mistake, Heidi still felt the need to leave her famous red notes telling us we made a mistake. We'd already noted that we had made a mistake. Was this really the best use of her time? Dispatchers did puzzles, read books, and just hung out. There was no consistent way of doing things from shift to shift.

Some dispatchers actually yelled at callers for calling 911! Others insisted on sending squad cars when none were required. The whole place was a mess, and Heidi was worried about spelling mistakes. I began to worry what would happen if a major incident took place in the county. What happened if we needed to evacuate the building? What happened when the angry dispatcher hung up on a caller who really needed help? Sometimes my coworkers fell asleep on the job. It was crazy, and the second shift hours did not help the situation. I lost confidence in the job based on constant derogatory questions from the sergeant on my shift! She seemed to belittle me on the radio. One example: I took a complaint about a boy riding a bicycle on the freeway. I sent a squad car to check on it. The sergeant actually got on the radio and asked me if I got a clothing description! Seriously? *Just look for the person riding a bicycle on the freeway!* How many callers driving by at 65 mph in the dark hours of the evening were able to give me a clothing description? She was hard on all new dispatchers, and I knew I just needed time to earn her respect. I was told she did not care for any female dispatchers at all. Oh, well.

And then there was Jim, the young firefighter who was interested in me. We texted often (or maybe I should say "sexted"), but every time we planned to get together he came up with some lame excuse for why he couldn't meet me. I couldn't believe I was desperate enough to be upset that a 22 year old canceled our plans for sex.

I was also on the dating service, Match.com. In the fall, I started seeing a man whom I met from that site. I managed to make it through the first date without sleeping with him, thanks to the pattern I had recognized with my new therapist. The second date was another story. We ended up going on three or four more dates. Up until then, he always drove an hour north from where he lived to see me. Finally, he wanted me to come down to him. We met in a bar and had some food. He explained that we couldn't go back to his house, because he was remodeling the bathroom. Some alarms started going off in my head at this point, but I silenced them. We drove to another bar, but it was *really* cold outside—I seemed to be getting more intolerant of cold and noise, for some reason—so the last thing I wanted to do was go into another bar. We couldn't go back to his house, so we went to a hotel. We had sex—and it was *not* good. We slept at the hotel for the night, and said goodbye in the morning. The next time we talked, we both agreed it was time to call it quits. I knew I had screwed this one up myself by making it just about sex. I felt like an idiot. On the other hand, the sex wasn't any good, so I didn't feel much sense of loss. I did like his physique, though!

Around October, one of my closest friends reported to me that she had been in the same bar where I had been drugged. Like me, she had consumed only two drinks and then remembered nothing. She woke up the next morning in her former apartment. The current resident was out of town. Somehow, somebody must have looked at her driver's license and drove her to that address. She had no idea how she got to the house or inside of it. Upon hearing this, I knew I had to report my rape to our Narcotics Unit so that no other women ended up in the same situation. I called the head of the unit and told him that I needed to speak with him about something important, but I didn't want to be seen speaking to him at work. He and another detective came to my home and I told them about both incidents. It was awful, and I felt so ashamed. To add insult to injury, I was asked to speak with the female detective the next time I was in the office. It turned out they were investigating a number of these cases. I told her what happened and explained that the man whom I believe drugged me was not the man who came to my home. I told her the man who drugged me used to be an employee at the bar in question, and that I knew his first name. A couple of times, the detective discreetly brought pictures to show me in dispatch, but they were never the right guy. I was mortified.

PART 5

A Spiral Down

"Our greatest glory is not in never falling,
but in getting up every time we do." ~ **Confucius**

chapter 32

Falling like a Brick

My depression began to escalate, but I never told anyone except Christine. I felt like a loser, because I couldn't use positive thinking and the Law of Attraction to snap myself out of this. I couldn't drag myself out of bed in the morning to get to the gym before work. I missed the guys with whom I used to work out every day between 4:00 and 6:00 p.m. At least they held me accountable for showing up, and we would all give each other a hard time. I also missed my friends and family. It was hard to keep in contact working opposite shifts. I slept too much and did too little. In early November, I felt suicidal but refused to think about it or act on it. Then, when I got my period, I told Christine, "Next month when I'm all out of whack like that again, remind me that I'm PMSing."

At work, I felt like things were going well. My supervisor and the sheriff approved of the work I was doing, and finally I earned some respect from Sgt. Margo. She even did the unthinkable and took me on my third ride-along herself! That was almost unheard of. That night, I felt like we'd come to an understanding of each other and that things would be better going forward. She'd even shared a little of herself with me.

I started seeing a psychologist in mid-2008 when the depression first took hold. I went on a common anti-depressant, Zoloft. Unfortunately, the longer I worked at the dispatch center, the more depressed I became. I slept almost all of the time that I wasn't at work. If I wasn't asleep, I was reclining on the couch staring at the TV.

It wasn't that I didn't like the job itself; I trusted almost nobody in the building. Early on after becoming employed there, I had a conversation with the third-shift training officer. She and I were the only people in the room at the time. Shortly after our conversation, the two other third shift dispatchers were reprimanded for certain behaviors. They began treating me with obvious disdain. The training officer told me that someone had told management what we talked about. Since only the two of us were in the room, and I knew I didn't tell management, it became obvious what had happened. Not only did that training officer tell management, she also told two other dispatchers that I had told on them. But the training officer was in denial, and she actually tried to convince me that listening devices were planted in the room! My greatest grievance was that I didn't like the lazy attitude of my supervisors, and the lack of preparedness for any major emergency. I finally convinced Capt. Bruss and Heidi to allow me to work with Jack, the senior training officer, to create a proper Policy & Procedure Manual. In addition to combining all of the material in the training binder and the memos, I had already reviewed policy manuals from dispatch centers of various sizes across the country, and I picked the format that best fit our needs. Jack and I mapped out the basic format of the book, and we started writing policies. We told Heidi that we would save every policy we wrote into a folder on the hard drive. Heidi simply needed to read them and give her approval, or tell us what direction she wanted us to go. I was anxious and excited about getting this project done. I looked forward to the improvements it would make on overall morale by providing some consistency. I wrote about a dozen policies in a couple of shifts, and I also created a "Call Taker's Checklist," based on an example from the *National Center for Missing and Exploited Children's Handbook*. (I had attended a training class hosted by that center, and the staff strongly recommended this guide. Because the guide was not available for distribution, it was up to us to create our own.) No matter how hard I tried, I simply could not convince Heidi to read—or implement—anything I had written. Finally, I gave up. I informed Capt. Bruss that I would not be writing any more policies, procedures, or guides until they were up to speed on what had already been done and let me know if what was written was what they wanted.

I continued to sink further into my depression. By early December, I thought about suicide every single day. On December 6, 2008, I wrote my suicide letter. It was a simple note blaming nobody for my actions; I could no longer handle my life and my pain. When I finished writing that letter, it was almost 3:00 p.m. I realized that if I attempted to kill myself then, there was a chance I may not be dead when the department sent a squad to check on me. That was standard procedure when someone didn't show up for work. I went to work pretending like nothing was wrong. I had a fine shift and talked to Kyle for a short time afterwards. He was the one I needed to be the most careful around. I could tell he was aware that something was different with me, and he was trying to figure out what was going on. He wouldn't hesitate to place me in protective custody if he thought I was a danger to myself.

On December 7, I sat and watched the Packer game, thinking about "doing it" the entire time. I even knew which drugs I would use. I had three drugs in the house that caused drowsiness and eventually decreased the body's ability to breathe. I mixed them all together and stared at them for a very long time. Finally, I said to myself, "You've wanted to do this every day for a while now. If you don't do it now, you'll still want to do it tomorrow." With that thought, I began taking as many pills as I could swallow at one time. I kept going until they were all gone. I thought that I would just fade off to sleep, and my troubles would be over. As you read in Chapter One, that's not what happened!

chapter 33

Life in "The Bin"

I was moved to the Mental Health Unit of the hospital just one day
after being taken off of the ventilator. I was certain that this would
likely cost me my job. Surprisingly, as I was brought in to the psych ward,
I was told that Capt. Bruss came to see me. It was *very* rare for him to leave
the office during the day. The hospital broke the rules by letting him see
me, because guests are not allowed before or after visiting hours. I guess he
had some pull, being captain of the county sheriff's department. He was
very calm as we sat and talked. I couldn't give him a logical explanation
as to why I had done it. I couldn't even understand that part myself. I was
still very fuzzy from whatever drugs they had given me in the Intensive
Care Unit, and I don't remember much about our conversation except that
when our conversation was over, I felt a lot better about the possibility of
keeping my job. Then, I became extremely resentful for having to attend
"group therapy."

I made my way into the first session and immediately noticed that
"cliques" existed even in the Psych Ward. A woman named Myra seemed
extremely loving towards the others. She claimed to be hospitalized for
alcoholism, but I suspected there was a whole lot more to it. The woman
who appeared to be her closest friend that first day was gone by dinner. I
quickly learned that was the way of the ward. Myra also was friends with
a man whom we all called "Paul the Pill Popping Plumber." I learned to
hang out with the alcoholics and addicts, because they were the most lucid
bunch in the place. Two women in the ward were bipolar and were clearly

improperly medicated or not medicated at all. They seemed perfectly normal one minute, and then they became combative or started talking to voices in their heads the next. A kind elderly woman was struggling with getting older. She said she'd been "losing it" for a while before she finally stood up in front of her family and said, "If somebody doesn't do something soon, I'm going to kill myself." I asked for her name, and then I remembered being the dispatcher who took that call. I had difficulty getting her family to tell me exactly what the issue was—something to the effect that "my wife's not right." It took a number of probing questions to determine that she was at least conscious and breathing. Finally, there was a man in the group named Tom who had *extreme* social anxiety. He only attended a few sessions, and even then I sensed his anxiety. I felt sorry for him and tried to comfort him whenever I could.

On the ward, we were free from scheduled activities and had visiting hours just after lunch at 1:00 p.m., and in the evening at 7:00. Sadly, most of the patients had no visitors. My parents and Christine arrived promptly at the start of visiting hours with candy, treats, and clothes for me. The staff was required to search and approve everything brought in. Belts, and anything with strings, were not permitted. Ironically, nobody checked for a belt when I came in, and I was still wearing it to hold my pants up. That first visiting hour was *so* difficult. My parents cried so much and I could not give them a rational explanation for what I'd done. My father talked about all of the things in his life that he could never have enjoyed again if I had died. We shared so many things. Then Dad came up with a quote that made us all laugh; it was repeated many times later. He said, "You've sure lowered the bar on our expectations for you. Now all you have to do to make us happy is just breathe." I was both laughing and crying. I knew my family had always expected great things from me and were always proud of me. If I had died, I knew Dad never would have listened to country music or watched another water-ski show in his lifetime. How could I have put them through this? Through everything, Christine was my rock. She never cried. She told me that she had called Noah, and he was very angry with me. He didn't know if he should get on a plane or not. She told him I was stable and there was no need to fly in. Christine wasn't sure when he'd be ready to talk. That didn't surprise me at all. Noah always was a "black and white, tell it like it is" kind of guy. I knew he viewed what I had done with the same degree of judgment as the "old me" would have viewed it.

Kyle never let me down. He called me on the first day I went to the mental health unit. When I answered his call, I said, "Kyle, I'm so sorry." He simply said, "I know." With those two simple words, I knew it was going to be okay. He called every day. Even his wonderful wife Laura talked with me on the phone. She said things like, "Bridgette, tell Kyle to move the refrigerator for me." We laughed, because we both knew he'd do it for her anyway. He may have been an alpha male at work, but at home Laura clearly ran the show. I often laughed about this with both of them.

My roommate was a *very* unhappy woman named Edna. During my first night there, I had a horrific cough due to the rapid intubation (quick insertion of a breathing tube) done in the emergency room and being on the ventilator for two days. I sucked on a cough drop continuously, and Edna complained about the smell. The staff checked on me every ten to fifteen minutes. By about the fourth round, Edna yelled, *"Why do you keep coming in here?!"* The social worker explained to Edna that she had a suicidal roommate and that the staff needed to monitor her very closely. I just pretended to be asleep. Eventually, I gave up on sleep and went out in the hall to stretch. I knew the camera was watching me, but they let me be. It felt good to stretch my legs and back. Then I went to the nurse's station and asked for something for pain and sleep. They gave me Ambien and Tylenol. Sweet relief! I finally managed to sleep.

In the morning, it was hard to believe I'd only been there one day! Each day seemed like weeks. I settled in at the breakfast table next to Paul while facing the entrance to the unit. At one point, I heard the nurses buzz someone in. I looked up and saw a deputy with whom I had worked for years. He was also a police officer in my village, so we worked together on fire and rescue calls. One time, I took care of him when he was injured while chasing a suspect. I immediately turned my head away, hoping my hair covered my face. I prayed he wouldn't see me. By now, I was sure every EMS worker in the county knew what I had done. But it was different having them actually see me there. Paul was not helpful. He drew even more attention to me by trying to cover my face with his food tray. The deputy was there to pick up the bipolar woman for court. I watched as they handcuffed and shackled her for transport. I thought that was unnecessary, as she could barely walk, and I rarely understood her speech. As soon as they left, one of the staff members rushed over to me to apologize. She said, "I'm so sorry. We forgot where you work. From now on, we will warn you before we buzz any law enforcement officers in." It was a little late now.

The day continued with endless sessions of "group therapy." We did talk therapy, arts and crafts, goal setting, and a nighttime session of goal evaluation. At first, I greatly resented arts and crafts; I have always hated them. Then I discovered a very cool and soothing kit to create "sun catchers." You poured paint into frames, and when it dried, it looked like stained glass. I found it relaxing and made a number of them while I was there.

The bipolar woman returned from court around lunchtime, and for the first time, I clearly understood her speech. I commented on the fact that they had handcuffed and shackled her. What she said next made me laugh uncontrollably. In her almost indiscernible voice, she said, "Yeah. Last time I tried to run. I got to the edge of the parking lot, but then I got lost." This came from a woman who, just earlier, was barely able to walk or speak!

My parents and Christine came to see me during visiting hours every day. Christine even laughed that they were now giving her an employee discount in the hospital cafeteria. My brothers also came now and then during the lunchtime visiting hour. Often, we had a hard time finding a place large enough for all of us to meet. One day, we all went to my room. Edna was gone, and I expected a new roommate shortly. I sat on the bed, and my family and friends all sat in chairs or on window sills. They asked why the worker came in every fifteen minutes, and I explained that they were required to write down my whereabouts and status that often.

It was hard to believe that I had been there for only two days! It felt like I'd been there for weeks! I mastered the ordering of meals. You had to place your order by 3:00 p.m. for the next day. You had to remember to order condiments, or you didn't get them. The food was surprisingly good, and I was growing comfortable there. It was easy. I didn't have to face the world or make hard choices. I didn't have to worry about the pile of unpaid bills at home, or the loan that Noah and his wife gave me just six months ago to help me pay off my debts. I didn't have to figure out how to make ends meet, as the salary I earned was so much less than what I earned when I bought the house. I didn't have to ask my parents for money to help me pay my bills. I didn't have to face the fact that life had just gotten too hard. Depression made *everything* hard. It almost paralyzed me. I wasn't able to solve problems or work through things the way I used to.

I grew tired of all of the visiting hours, because it felt like so much work; I just wanted some time to do nothing at all. Paul was released early on day two and was quickly replaced by Scott. Scott also was an alcoholic, but he was kind and more peaceful. He talked about his family a lot and how he wanted to be a better parent to his children. I actually kept his email address for a while. When he stopped emailing, I knew it was because he had relapsed and did not want to tell me. I said as much in my next email, and he said I was right. At the time I wrote this, I didn't know the fate of any of the people I encountered there.

Emergency detention was a 72-hour hold from the time you arrived in the Mental Health Unit. When 72 hours were up, patients saw the psychiatrist, and he determined whether you were fit for release or needed to stay longer. If he determined that you needed to stay, a court appearance was scheduled, just like the one the bipolar woman went to on day one. I eagerly waited my turn to see the doctor on Friday, hoping I could go home. If he didn't see me Friday, it would be Monday before I could see him again. Fortunately, I saw him on Friday afternoon, and I was cleared for release. I was going home! Friday was the one day Kyle didn't call me. I'd wondered why when the social worker showed me an article in the newspaper about our SWAT team being out all night on a call. I was relieved to know that it had ended well, and that explained the lack of a call. (Kyle later told me he didn't call that day because he wasn't sure I wanted to talk to him. He said I always seemed quiet and rushed. I explained that the patient phone was very public and there were a lot of people always waiting to use it.)

During one visiting hour, my parents informed me that my cousin Colleen was flying in from Atlanta to spend a few days with me. Honestly, I loved Colleen and was happy to see her—any other time. I *so* looked forward to being home alone with my two cats. I wasn't ready to face the world just yet.

chapter 34

You Can't Hide Forever

Christine picked me up from the hospital while my parents met Colleen at the airport. It was the strangest feeling walking to the car and riding home. I felt like ducking down in the car, as if there was a neon sign with an arrow pointing right at me, saying "crazy woman!" Christine and I laughed when I collected the clothing I wore when I was taken to the hospital. I said to her, "You really let me out of the house like this?" Christine explained that I had no socks on, so she grabbed my red footie comfy socks and put them on me. She also grabbed a random jacket out of my closet—one that was about four sizes too big. What a sight that must have been! I certainly had my sense of humor back!

As soon as we got to my home, Mom and Dad arrived with Colleen. Everybody stayed for a while, and then Colleen and I were left to our own devices. I wasn't in the mood to do anything except sit on the couch and watch TV. I told Colleen some of the rules from "the (loony) bin," like the fact that you were not allowed to have dental floss. I said, "How in the hell would somebody kill themselves with dental floss?" We laughed hard when the cop show we just happened to be watching involved a man who hung himself with a noose made of dental floss!

The next morning, practically my entire family—Mom, Dad, some brothers, Christine, Colleen—arrived for brunch. I was terrified to leave the house for fear of running into people I knew. I was sure that they had all heard about it by now. But brunch went off without a hitch. That was comforting. Colleen must have been bored to tears, because I really did not feel like doing anything that weekend. However, I had an appointment to go in to work on Monday to meet with Capt. Bruss and the sheriff. One of the most difficult things I have *ever* done in my life was holding my head up, getting out of my car, and walking into that building! Our meeting went smoothly. They explained that I had to see the department psychologist to be cleared for duty. As a result, the earliest I could expect to return to work was after Christmas. I was told that the sheriff's administrative assistant would make the appointment and call me to let me know when it was.

Although not working for a while meant even more financial hardship, I knew there was nothing I could do about it. So I decided to enjoy my time off. I returned home and found Colleen, Mom and Dad waiting to take me to lunch—another outing where I was likely to see people I knew. I was still quite nervous about that! We went to a local pub and ordered burgers. Thus far, the only people I knew were the pub workers, and that didn't bother me. I was worried about seeing other firefighters, EMTs, or police officers. We finished eating and were about to leave when I ran into a very kind man from the fire department. He also was my home maintenance man. He talked to me a bit, and it was clear that he had not heard what happened. If he hadn't heard, there was a good chance a lot of people hadn't.

Mom and Dad took Colleen back to the airport after lunch, and I was finally able enjoy solitude for what seemed like the first time in months. Actually, only a week had passed. I looked forward to some peace in the home that I loved with my cats. I *loved* nighttime when it became deadly quiet in my house. I heard an occasional car drive by, but that was it. My solitude was going to have to wait, though. For the entire first week after I returned home, I was in almost hourly phone contact with at least one member of my family. I knew that if I failed to answer the phone, everyone would go into panic mode, so I made sure to always carry a phone with me. My brothers also stopped in, one by one. It didn't escape my notice that none of their wives did. I couldn't blame them. One particularly disturbing visit was from my brother Rodney. He brought his two grandchildren—ages 5 and 9—with him. When my brother wasn't around, my great-niece whispered to me: "Grandpa told us you've been sick, but my Mom told me what really happened. She just doesn't want Grandpa to know she told me." I was so stunned! I've always loved her mother unconditionally as if she were my own child, despite the fact that, as she'd grown older, she was no longer affectionate towards me at all. I spent almost all of my free time with her from the time she was born until they moved away around the time she was 7. I could not believe she told her own child that Aunt Bridgette tried to kill herself!

Once I had a chance to enjoy my solitude, and could actually talk at length on the phone, Kyle called to see how I was. This conversation gave me a glimpse of what he had gone through as a result of my actions. My friend and colleague Brad contacted Kyle, who spent that first night with my family. Thankfully, by the time he arrived at the hospital, Sgt. Margo had left. Then, when he finished his shift the following morning, one of the first shift deputies asked Kyle if he had heard that I tried to kill myself last night. He acknowledged that he'd heard. The deputy then told him that there had been a suicide note—and his name was in it! Poor Kyle had to live with not knowing anything more about the note until we were finally able to talk. I told him that I had left a note, but his name was nowhere in it. Then Kyle proceeded to ask me a lot of hard questions, such as: "Did you try to tell me? Was there anything I missed? Why did you do it? And was there anything I should have said or done that could have prevented this?" I answered all of his questions as honestly as I could. I told him I had not tried to tell anyone. I was ashamed of my depression and hid it well. There was nothing anyone could have said or done. My brain just ceased to function correctly. It was a very healing conversation for me. Many months later, as I drove home from work, I first heard the Rascal Flatts song, "Why," on the radio. I had to pull my car over and cry. Listening to that song made me realize that Kyle had been the only one to ask me the hard questions. Everyone else just tiptoed around me—*and* the issue. I began to realize that that's how my family handled every issue; we just pretended it didn't exist.

After being home for a couple of weeks, things quieted down and I had nothing but time on my hands. I decided to create a "family book" as a Christmas gift for my parents. I asked all of my brothers, sisters-in-law, nieces, and nephews to send me quotes, stories, and wisdom that they had received from my parents. I designed their responses into varying blocks of colors, fonts and cutouts, and put them into a scrapbook. The project involved more time and effort than I had expected, but it certainly paid off! Mom and Dad were so in love with the book. It was as if it was the best thing in the whole world.

The day came when I was scheduled to meet with the department shrink. I expected the session would consist of an hour of sitting on a couch, talking about what I'd done and how I resolved to never do it again. Instead, I was given a *huge* batch of tests. One test alone was 1,000 questions, but I "only" had to complete the first 300. When we talked, the psychologist came at me hard with such simple questions as, "Did you attempt to kill yourself?" Well, let me think: "Yes." Then, "Were you placed on a ventilator?" Again, "Yes." Throughout the interrogation, I thought, "Does he expect me to deny it? I'm sure he has all of my records." He informed me that he would send his recommendation to the sheriff immediately.

chapter 35

Breathe In, Breathe Out

I didn't expect to return to work until after Christmas, but I was called in to see Capt. Bruss and the sheriff a few days before Christmas. I typed up a letter that I wanted to share with my colleagues before I returned to work. The captain wasn't sure about this, but the sheriff was all for it. Basically, I wanted to address the "elephant in the room" before I was back, so things weren't quite as awkward when I saw everyone again. In the letter, I explained that I had attempted suicide. Doctors determined that it was the result of an imbalance of chemicals and hormones in my brain, and that I was now stable. I wrote to my colleagues that I still had the same dark sense of humor, so they didn't have to tiptoe around me and avoid phrases like "that's crazy!" I also wrote that I had nothing to hide, and if anyone wanted to ask me any questions, they were more than welcome to. I was invited to come back to work on Christmas Eve! Really? Fortunately, I was moved to the day shift on Christmas Eve, so I didn't have to miss my family Christmas.

The drive in to work was hard, and I dreaded my arrival! It took every ounce of courage I had to breathe deeply before getting out of my car. I almost turned around and ran back to my car about five times. I walked in as if it was just another day. I said hello to Heidi and my fellow dispatchers. The day shift sergeant was in the dispatch center when I arrived. He said, "Welcome back. I'm sure it couldn't have been easy to come in here." I never appreciated two sentences more! It certainly helped to take the edge off. I could tell that my fellow dispatchers tiptoed around me a bit. All I could do was be me, so I tried to make them comfortable.

As I got back into the second shift swing, I was so grateful for Kyle. He stopped in every night before he went to the squad room just to say "hi." At least I knew I had one ally in the department. Every night as I got into in my car, he pulled his squad car out and we parked next to each other and chatted a bit. Those talks helped me decompress and always made me feel better.

When I did return for my first full shift, Sgt. Margo was not ready to forgive me. I put apology/thank you cards, along with a box of chocolates, in the in-boxes down in the squad room for both her and Brad, and also for the dispatchers who worked that night. She immediately mentioned the chocolates and said she could not accept them. I said, "Well then, just leave them in the squad room for the guys." She ignored me and walked out. From that moment on, I knew the road to recovery would be long. I just had *no idea* just how long, or how rough!

Every single shift, Sgt. Margo challenged me, or complained about something. If I answered the phone when she called dispatch, she simply said, "Let me talk to your partner." It didn't matter who my partner was, as long as it wasn't me! The tension became almost unbearable, but I was determined not to let her break me.

Sometime in February, I was at work, just talking with a fellow dispatcher, when I suddenly had a horrific tearing pain in my throat. It was so bad I began cough and lost most of my ability to speak. I was worried. I immediately thought of the breathing tube and suspected that I might have torn a vocal cord. The immediate pain was bizarre and severe. I called the jail sergeant on duty and asked him to send an EMT to dispatch. One of the deputies came to my side, and I asked him look at my throat to see if he could see a tear or bleeding. He could not. I dialed the on-call doctor and asked if this condition was something that would get worse if I waited until morning to come in. She said it would not. The following morning, I called the doctor's office and was sent to the hospital so a scope could be placed down my throat. I was sedated during that process, so Christine came to the rescue again by driving me to the hospital. She even went up to visit with the ear, nose and throat specialist before I awoke from the procedure. He explained that I had a nodule on my vocal cord and was not allowed to speak *at all* until he said otherwise.

Based on your experience reading this book, you can probably tell that I like to talk. So, you can also guess how well *not speaking* worked for me. That's when I first ventured into the world of Facebook! My family and friends tried to get me to sign up for ages, but I didn't want to sit at a computer at home when I worked every night in front of four or more computer screens. Not being able to talk to anyone suddenly changed my mind. I was amazed at how many old friends I connected with immediately.

At first, the sheriff's department allowed me to work my normal shifts, but instructed the other dispatchers that I was not to answer any radio or phone calls and they were not to talk to me. I was charged with quality control of all injunctions—restraining orders—for the past few years. It was incredibly boring and tedious work! It was also difficult for me to not talk to anyone, but I ended up talking anyway. I was sent for speech therapy to learn how to speak properly. After a number of weeks, Heidi and Capt. Bruss determined that I was not getting any better. They put me on a forced leave until the ENT doctor released me for duty. I couldn't afford to be off of work, so I went to the doctor and begged him to release me. He did so on the condition that I not work more than eight hours at a time, and that I not talk between radio transmissions or phone calls. That didn't sit well with my senior colleagues, who were sometimes required to come in early or stay late.

Around the time when I was finally able to talk again, Sgt. Margo left work on a medical leave for a couple of months. That gave me the opportunity to get back into my groove without constant concern for what the "complaint of the day" would be. I began to enjoy my work again. The dispatcher who was hired around the same time as me was named Rochelle. She and I used to have so much fun working together when Sgt. Margo was not there to complain, and no other dispatchers were there to fill our heads with war stories and conspiracy theories. Sometimes, Rochelle and I just laughed and laughed during the whole shift. We always brought in treats on our "working together" nights, which usually came around once a week. We both looked forward to those nights. The other two second-shift dispatchers were so serious. One always complained or looked for things to complain about—and she was a *huge* conspiracy theory nut! (At least I thought so until the "target was painted on my back," as she claimed to have seen before.) Rochelle and I realized that we'd never actually seen her laugh. The other second shift dispatcher was Jack, the field training officer. Jack was never a bad guy to me.

Rochelle told me that Jack hated her. He told her at the beginning of her training that he did not want her hired. I don't know why he would ever have said that. I thought Jack was a good guy at heart. He kept following the carrot the department constantly dangled in front of him, which was a promotion. He believed he would either get Heidi's job when she retired, or that they would add a "lead dispatcher" position, freeing up Heidi to do administrative tasks. He played everything exactly by the book. But once I started talking about how much I liked Rochelle, and how great she was, Jack started to come around. On the nights when the three of us worked together, Jack actually started to have fun. We joked and said, "Come on, Jack! Come over to the dark side!"

chapter 36

Down Down Down

$\mathcal{S}$adly, the day came when Sgt. Margo returned to work. I avoided her as much as possible. We rotated assignments in dispatch and I tried to avoid working the county radio desk when she was working. No need to give her more things to pick apart. Once she returned, I began getting letters and notes in my mailbox almost daily. Every note had a call card marked with red ink by Heidi, asking why I did this or said that. I knew the complaints were coming from Sgt. Margo. The other second shift sergeant always told me the moment he didn't like something that I'd done, and I tried to not repeat the mistake. Sgt. Margo never addressed me directly. It always came from Heidi.

As the year went on, the complaints began to pile up. I was constantly being "talked to" about minor mistakes that did not result in any harm, errors that other dispatchers made regularly without notice. The situation reminded me very much of a 1980's film, *Sleeping with the Enemy*. In the film, an abused woman worked all day to ensure the house was spotless, even going so far as to alphabetize the pantry. When her husband came home, he claimed that one of the hand towels in the powder room was slightly crooked, so he beat the snot out of her. I was never worried about putting anyone in danger or getting anyone hurt, but every single shift I had to worry about what the "hand towel" was going to be. Finally, I advised Heidi and Capt. Bruss that I was being singled out as a result of my suicide attempt. When my first two emails garnered no response, I copied the sheriff and human resources on my next email. I made it clear that Sgt.

Margo, and now Heidi, were singling me out. I believed it was due to my suicide attempt, and that I would no longer tolerate such discrimination. I finally heard from the captain, who scheduled me for a meeting on October 27, 2009. I notified the union representative and sought legal counsel. I went into that meeting and followed the instructions of my lawyer. I said a complaint was being filed with the Equal Employment Opportunity Commission, because Sgt. Margo and later Heidi had singled me out. When the sheriff asked what I wanted to come out of this complaint, I said I simply wanted them to talk to Sgt. Margo and then I would withdraw my complaint. They refused to do that. They said that she was the shift supervisor, and it was her job to report on the performance of all employees on that shift. I advised them that I had no choice but to proceed with my complaint. Other employees told me that this was just the way it was in the department. Nobody knew exactly what kind of hold Sgt. Margo had over the senior officers or the sheriff, but I was told that she would *never* be talked to or reprimanded. For once, the gossip was correct. I asked coworkers what happened to previous employees who had complained, and I was always told, "Nobody's ever made it this far. They've either withdrawn their complaint or they've quit."

When I arrived for work the following shift, I was immediately called into Heidi's office and was told that due to the unusually high number of mistakes I'd made (going all the way back to my start date, using incidents that were never even mentioned in the review from my probationary period), I was to spend at least two additional shifts with Jack for "remedial training." If this wasn't retaliation for my complaints, then I don't know what it was! I found it ironic that they claimed my performance was so poor that I needed additional training, and yet they trusted me enough to be the senior dispatcher in the room with Rochelle until the added training was scheduled later that week. I almost wished something bad had happened on those shifts just so my supervisors would have been held liable. By now, I was taking Diazepam every day just to calm down enough to walk into the building.

The night came when I was to work with Jack. I was so furious, because I talked with Jack almost every shift. I asked him to offer constructive feedback if he saw the need. During my "remedial training," we talked about the issues I was working on—geography on the northern end of the county, and slowing down my response to critical calls. When the shit hit the fan on an urgent call, I tended to air the information as soon as I knew what I had. I was supposed to slow down, gather more information, and specifically address the deputy assigned to that area as opposed to just airing it to all squads. Jack, and the "good sergeant" as I referred to him, talked with me about that and I was working on it. It was ironic that Sgt. Margo didn't know I was working with Jack that night. She called to complain about something I'd done. When she asked for Jack, I said, "He's on the line." She said, "Okay, have him call me." She hung up before I could explain that he was on the line with us, because he was "training" me. She had two complaints that night. When she told them to Jack, he explained that he was on the line with me and had either directed or approved of my decisions. In one case, she was at an accident scene and had asked for a second flatbed. I was dialing one, but Jack instructed me to just ask the first truck if he could take both vehicles. Sgt. Margo was pissed that I'd done this, but when she found out it was Jack's decision, it was suddenly not worth complaining about. Miraculously, there were no complaints to Heidi that shift.

As things continued to deteriorate, it became clear that they were either trying to make me quit or find cause to fire me. My union rep said her hands were tied, because what they were doing wasn't "official disciplinary action." My lawyer was either unreachable or not very much help.

chapter 37

Going Going Gone

On December 11, 2009, I took a call about 11:45 p.m. from a scared young man who was upside down in a truck in a remote location. His friend, the driver, was pinned with his legs behind his head. I immediately aired this information to the third shift sergeant because it was shift change and all of the squads were still in the station. Once I aired the information to get squads moving, I asked Rochelle to page fire and rescue. I stayed online with the caller, gathering as much information as possible while trying to keep him calm and conscious. At one point, he wanted to try and move his friend, but I kept him from doing so. I continually updated the responding squads on any new information I received from the injured man. As soon as the fire chief came on the radio, I shared as much information as possible, allowing him to determine the need for Jaws of Life, a paramedic intercept, and a helicopter before he ever arrived on scene. Those resources were immediately dispatched. As a dispatcher, I was not allowed to tell fire departments what they would need. As the only dispatcher who was also a firefighter/EMT, I *could* give them the information they needed to make that determination on their own. Because of this, the driver gained a good twenty minutes in the golden hour of life—the time period offering the highest likelihood that prompt medical treatment will prevent death or permanent disability. I turned the call over to the third shift dispatchers and left work feeling like I did a good job. This was confirmed the following day when the county medical director stopped into dispatch to thank me for a job well done. She told me that the information I provided was invaluable in getting advanced life support to that young man in a timely manner.

However, when I came in for my next shift, the call card was in my box with a letter. Capt. Bruss and Heidi wanted me to explain my decision to not "simulcast" the call to our squads, along with fire and rescue. On a regular fire and rescue call, we pushed a button that transmitted the fire and rescue page to our squads, as well. I explained that our squads were in the garage, so I gave them the information the moment I knew we had something serious. I had my partner confirm jurisdiction and page fire and rescue while I stayed online with the caller and updated responding squads.

The *next* shift, Rochelle got the note in her box. They asked her why it took eight minutes from the time I answered the call to the time fire and rescue were paged. I was furious. This was the second attempt to find flaw in the handling of that call—and now they were going after Rochelle! It took a long time for me to listen to, and document, the times recorded on both the phone line and the radio lines, but eventually I was able to prove the error was in the recording equipment and not in the response time. I demonstrated that it took only three minutes from the moment I said, "911 where's your emergency," to when fire and rescue were paged and en-route.

When I came in for my next shift, I was called into Capt. Bruss's office, along with Heidi. The two of them wanted to know why I allowed my partner to page fire and rescue instead of doing it myself. I explained that I was on the line with a critical caller and she was not occupied with a call at the time. I saw this situation as an example of teamwork rather than something to find flaw in. They responded, "Well, what if her phone rang?" I replied that if Rochelle had received a call, we would have changed plans, but it didn't. I clarified that they were telling me I should have put a critical 911 call on hold to page fire and rescue myself while my partner did nothing. They said yes. I told them I disagreed with that position 100 percent. I advised them to check the logs. If they had, they would've discovered that one dispatcher pages fire and rescue for another dispatcher at least two or three times a day. When I got back to my desk, I sent an email to Capt. Bruss and Heidi, with a copy to the sheriff, recapping what they had just told me. I noted that I thought it very inappropriate to discourage teamwork. I reiterated that if I had put that boy on hold and lost him, then I would have been responsible. He could have killed the driver had he attempted to move him. The call could have dropped before squads located the vehicle. The caller could have become unconscious and I would not have known about it. I wanted a paper trail, proof that they told me *not* to use teamwork. I called in sick on Saturday, January 6, because I just couldn't bring myself to go into work.

By now, I had secretly taken the time to figure out how someone could hang herself from a bathroom stall using a belt. That was my secret "out." I knew that if things got too bad, I could use this information. I called the county crisis manager. She had become a friend just before Christmas when I volunteered to help out a family suffering from depression or mental illness. She picked a family for me and gave me their Christmas list. My friends and family came together and provided an amazing Christmas for this family. That Saturday, when I called her, she came over and sat with me for a while and chatted about my current situation. I even told her about my "belt plan." When I went into work for my next shift on Sunday, January 7, 2010, I found a letter in my box from Capt. Bruss, claiming they were not "discouraging teamwork." He said it just wasn't warranted in this case. (If not this case, when?)

By this time, I had approached a suicidal state again. I knew that if my supervisors were trying this hard to find fault in a call that went well, I would be hung out to dry the next time a call didn't go well. I had already gone past the boiling point! January 7 was a Sunday, and no management was at work. We were allowed to wear jeans and Packer attire on Sundays. After receiving the letter in my box, I realized I didn't wear a belt to work that day. I called my friend, the crisis manager, and we talked about what was best for me. I then went downstairs to the sergeant's office. The "good sergeant" was working that night. I told him it had gotten to the point that I would rather kill myself than be at work. He said, "Be careful what you say. I don't want to have to chapter you." I said, "I'm not telling you I'm going to kill myself. I'm telling you I'm on medical leave, effective now." I went upstairs, said goodbye to the two other dispatchers, and never returned.

My psychologist signed off on my disability and I went the first 90 days with no pay. Thank goodness for the help of family during that time. I began collecting long-term disability insurance after the first 90 days.

chapter 38

My Dream Destroyed

I had started a new company the previous August, and viewed my leaving the department in January as an opportunity to get the business up and running. I sent out one mailing with no response and decided to wait until after returning from my February cruise to keep going.

A family member gifted me with a cruise that year, or I never could have gone. On that cruise, I was in an unusual amount of pain. I felt exhausted. A fabulous group of family and friends were traveling with us, and yet, I just couldn't keep up. Ironically, my family thought that I was depressed because this was the same ship I'd met Nathan on. In truth, I still cherished those memories. My time with the original Nathan (the person I had believed him to be) taught me much about what I wanted in a relationship. I held no ill will. I was in pain and tried to hide it. In the afternoon, most people were off doing their own thing. I snuck back to my cabin, ordered room service for lunch, and then napped until it was time to dress for dinner.

I had dinner with the group, and then I liked to go to the casino. I joined back up with my group for late-night entertainment—usually karaoke or game shows. On previous cruises, I was known to be in the nightclub until it closed. On this cruise, I was in bed by midnight most nights. I just hurt. I got a massage on the first day at sea, hoping it would help with the pain. Sadly, it didn't. I even got a second massage on day four or five. Massages on ships are *not* cheap, but I was willing to do anything to feel better.

When the cruise finally ended and I was back home, I fell into my bed and slept almost continuously for an entire week! That following Monday, I called my doctor's office and was given an appointment to see his physician's assistant. When she looked at my current symptoms, combined with all of my previous complaints of pain and fatigue, she put it all together. She believed I had fibromyalgia. All I knew about it was that there was no cure. She gave me some information and I left the office feeling shell-shocked. My first stop was a local bookstore where I picked up *The Idiot's Guide to Fibromyalgia,* and several other books. I immediately began to read everything I could get my hands on. As I read about the illness and the symptoms I could expect, I honestly felt angry that the condition wasn't fatal. At least then, I would get some relief. As horrible as that sounds now, that was how I felt at the time. I didn't foresee much chance at a real life with a body ravaged by illness.

By the time I saw my doctor again, I was familiar with standard treatment plans and current studies on fibromyalgia. We went through all of the remedial treatments. When they weren't working, I went in to his office one day with extreme hip pain. I'll never forget his words: "You have fibromyalgia! If it's not your hip, it will be something else. Fibromyalgia needs to be treated by a psychiatrist!" Clearly he hadn't read the latest studies that had proven fibromyalgia to be a central nervous system disorder, *not* a psychiatric condition!

I called my former boss at the preschool to ask for a doctor recommendation. She referred me to a very kind doctor named Dr. Nick. I scheduled an appointment and was surprised at how simple his office was. By the time I started seeing Dr. Nick, I had been in pain for so long that I just wanted someone to listen to me and understand. He appeared to really care. He set me up with a pain doctor and even came to a session with my psychologist.

After I'd been in to see him a couple of times and had called him in crisis, clearly Dr. Nick had decided I was a nut case. Against my better judgment, I still gave him a chance to try the normal fibromyalgia protocols. I called him numerous times on the weekend and I sensed that he thought I was overreacting to the pain. But that's the definition of fibromyalgia: overactive pain transmitters and receptors.

Doctor Danger

One night, the pain was so bad that I called Dr. Nick a few times, but I got no call back from him. I tried the pain doctor with the same result. I called Kyle, and I agreed to call a friend from the fire department named Mishka, who agreed to sit with me. If needed, she would request the squad to transport me to the hospital. Finally, I called my psychologist and left a message explaining to her that I was just in so much pain I couldn't take it anymore. I was looking for someone to advocate for me, because I knew I was going to the E.R. They have a history of judging patients with a psychiatric history and chronic pain as crazy, fakers or drug seekers. I was none of the above. Mishka, the wife of one of the fire chiefs, arrived and she could tell I was in severe pain; I was far more agitated than she'd ever seen me. She called her husband and asked him to send the rescue squad for me. When the page went out for rescue, Sgt. Margo heard it on her radio and recognized my address. She also decided to send a squad. Lucky for me, Kyle's unit happened to be the only squad available. He stepped into the rescue squad and grabbed my hand, reassuring me that I would get some relief soon. Since he already knew the situation, I didn't have to say much. He determined I was not a danger to myself or others, and he went on his way. As I've said time and again, Kyle has more integrity than anyone I know. He would not bend rules for me. If he thought I was in danger, he would be the first one to lock me up.

Upon arrival at the hospital, the doctor came right into the room. I sensed his venom before he even started speaking. He kept trying to get me to say I was suicidal. I kept telling him that I wasn't suicidal at the moment, but I was afraid it would become an issue if he couldn't break the pain cycle. I said, "I'm not a drug seeker! If you look at my chart, you'll see that the last doctor broke the cycle with Toradol (a pain reliever) and Ativan (to relieve anxiety)." As he left the room, he said in the most condescending voice possible, "I'll give you Toradol, but you're not getting Ativan!" I never saw him again—and I knew what was happening. They called the sheriff's department to have me placed on a Chapter 51 detention. When the doctor called Kyle, he explained that he knew me well and I was simply in a lot of pain. Break the pain cycle and remove the threat. The doctor apparently was not satisfied with this answer, so he went over Kyle's head to Sgt. Margo. No matter how much I explained to them that the pain was physical and not mental, they just wouldn't listen. Christine arrived at the hospital, and Mishka also was still there. They tried to keep me calm, but I wasn't. A short time later, one of my former colleagues, Duane, came into my room. At first I was relieved to see him. I said, "Duane, you have to help me. I'm not suicidal. I'm just in physical pain!" He advised me that it was out of his hands at this point. Sgt. Margo. I just knew it. I was being made to suffer for my sins. The nurse came in to give me a shot of Toradol and to take my IV out. I said, "That's it? He's not going to control my pain at all?" I could tell she felt bad about the whole situation. I told her I wouldn't have to come to the hospital for something as simple as Ativan, because I had my own Diazepam in my med bag. She quietly said to me, "Your med bag is right behind you on the cot." (Normally, for patients who are a risk for suicide, the hospital staff ensures that all meds are kept out of the room.) As she stepped out with the deputies, she closed the curtain behind her. This was the cue for Christine to reach into my med bag and grab my Diazepam. I took two before Duane came back in to put me in handcuffs and a belly chain. A second deputy arrived from the jail to assist in the transport. (Seriously? Was all of this really necessary? I was not a threat to anyone!) Duane explained that he was just following procedure. If nothing else, Duane was one to do it by the book. No beds were available in the Mental Health Unit at the hospital, so I was being transported to another hospital thirty minutes away! At some point, I heard my father yelling in the hallway. My father does *not* yell! He was so furious, because they were not letting him see me. I'm not sure if he did it out of professional courtesy or because my dad was making such a scene, but Duane did let my dad in to see me for just a minute. I was bawling, and he was crying. He yelled at Duane and I explained to him that Duane had no choice in the matter. I urged him not to yell. This was one of the worst moments of my life. I was paraded through the ER in handcuffs and chains, past all of the people I used to call friends or colleagues. I was put in the back of the squad car. I lay sideways and cried all the way to the second hospital. Neither Duane nor the other deputy even acknowledged me—or my pain—the entire way.

It seemed like forever since I'd first gone to the E.R. looking for pain relief. Now, I was being searched and processed in the psych ward of a new hospital. It was at least 3:00 a.m. when I was settled into my room. A doctor came in to see me an hour later, but she was just a medical doctor. I needed to see the psychiatrist if I was to be released. I woke up numerous times that night and hardly slept at all. The staff planned to let me sleep, due to my late arrival, but I figured if I couldn't sleep, I might as well participate in the group sessions. At least *that* might take my mind off of the pain. In every group session, I expressed how angry I was that I was there at all. I finally got to see the psychiatrist at 5:00 p.m. As soon as he heard my story, he authorized my immediate release. I had been detained for more than 24 hours after I initially sought help for the pain. At least I could double up my usual dose of pain meds. When I called my father to pick me up, he cried with relief.

Once I was released from that hospital, I was still in pain. I continued to call Dr. Nick for answers. One day, the pain was so bad that I called his office numerous times. His assistant finally told me to come in at 5:00 p.m. When I did, Dr. Nick told me that he had talked with my psychologist and pain doctor and they were all in agreement that I had been misdiagnosed. He said I had something more than just fibromyalgia and depression—a much deeper psychological issue that required inpatient care for a while. Imagine hearing *that* from your doctor! I felt betrayed. If I needed more psychiatric treatment, wouldn't my therapist of two years have mentioned that at some point? I drove home crying—and in shock. I called my parents to come up and sit with me, because I was *now* in danger of returning to a suicidal state. Had there been a convenient bridge between the doctor's office and home, I might have just driven off of it. Thankfully, there was not. I also called the county crisis manager and discussed this with her. While she didn't feel I was a danger, she did say that I had been on so many different medications for so long, nobody even knew where my baseline was anymore. She suggested that, if I was an inpatient, they could do what is called a "med wash." That involved taking me off of all of my medications in a very controlled environment. I decided that I wanted answers, and if my doctors thought I needed inpatient treatment, I would do it. I didn't want to keep switching doctors until I found one who would tell me what I wanted to hear. As I talked with Mom and Dad, we agreed I would try it. I still felt they were wrong, but I would do what they asked. The next morning, I shopped for pajamas and comfy clothes with no drawstrings, and some slippers. I called my psychologist's office to find out what hospital I should report to. They wanted me to go to a mental health hospital in Milwaukee. I called the hospital, but they had never heard of me. I answered some questions, and then they transferred me to someone who began telling me about an outpatient program. I explained that my doctors told me I needed to be inpatient. They said that the doctor had to call and order it. I called the psychologist's office and the staff said to call the hospital back in ten minutes. I redialed the hospital. Now they had heard of me, but they didn't want to admit me. Throughout the week, I *tried* to follow my doctor's orders, but no psychiatric hospital wanted to admit me. I called the facility where I was taken on the night of my living hell. I explained my situation to the unit director, and he said it sounded like I should be admitted. He said they had an open bed, but I should go to the ER first. And so, Mom and Dad picked me up and took me to the hospital. After I talked to the doctors in the ER, they consulted with the on-call psychiatrist, who decided I did not need to be an inpatient.

That week I made numerous calls to my doctor and psychologist, explaining that I was *trying* to follow orders, but nobody would admit me. I made a ton of calls and even went to hospital intake centers. None of them thought I needed admission. Finally, I was so stressed and tired of it all that I called on my friend, the county crisis manager. I told her I needed a ride and a bed. She drove me to the hospital in my area for medical clearance and then to the other hospital where a bed was waiting for me. I told them I was suicidal due to the stress of my doctors and my pain issues. I was admitted and stayed there for 10 days.

On my first day there, I attended a group therapy session with a man who looked oddly familiar. In the discussions, he began talking about how he'd just been in jail and had now turned undercover informant for the sheriff's department. I thought to myself, "Oh shit! I bet that's where I saw him." I used to walk through the jail on my breaks and stop to talk to the jail sergeant and one of the deputies. It caused a stir among those incarcerated, because my uniform was a white shirt (the same worn by lieutenants and captains) and I was a woman. Now I was in the psych ward with one of those inmates! Later, I discreetly approached the nurse and said, "I don't want you to break any confidentiality rules, but this man was just in jail and I need to know if it was *my* jail. That would put me in a dangerous position." Glass walls no longer separated us. Fortunately, that undercover informant was released that same day and I didn't need to worry. In addition to attending group therapy sessions and seeing the psychiatrist, I was allowed to see a pain doctor and physical therapist. Later in my stay, I met a guy who *had* been suicidal and was brought in by *my* department. He told me he was not handcuffed, was allowed to talk on his cell phone the whole time, and was transported by a lone female officer. I was furious. I was much smaller than the deputies and was known to them, but I was chained and cuffed and required two deputies. That guy was *huge* and could have done some damage! He wasn't cuffed, and required only one deputy. Where was the justice in that? I was released from the hospital after ten days with a diagnosis of (are you ready for this?) fibromyalgia and depression!

PART 6

Transformation

"When you do things from your soul,
you feel a river moving in you, a joy." ~ **Rumi**

chapter 40

Facing Facts

I never saw any of those doctors again. Even the psychologist I'd been seeing for close to three years now had betrayed me. She either agreed with Dr. Nick's assessment or she didn't. If she agreed, she should have called in orders to have me admitted. If she didn't agree, she should have told him and me exactly that!

I remembered seeing a classmate at my 20th high school reunion the previous summer. She was now a family practice doctor in my area. I knew her as kind and compassionate person. I planned to make an appointment with her when the weekend was over.

In addition to finding a new doctor at my reunion, I also saw my childhood friend Donny. Donny had grown up to be a happy family man. However, he had a number of serious illnesses and eventually required a liver transplant. I was kept informed of his progress by my parents. I also was on Donny's email list, because he hosted an annual party at his beautiful home. He received his transplant just months before the reunion. I was shocked that he not only made it to the reunion, but looked great! I told him so. Then Donny told me that he heard that I'd been very ill, as well. At that moment, I felt an incredible sense of guilt! My parents had not told their friends the real reason I had been in the hospital. They just told them that I'd had a drug reaction and was on a ventilator. (Yes, most people would react to swallowing three bottles of drugs, so I guess it wasn't a complete lie.) Here, Donny fought to live for so long, while I had tried to die. At that moment, I didn't even feel worthy of being in his presence.

When the day came for my first scheduled appointment with my high school classmate, she was gone on an emergency. I was forced to see another doctor, who just happened to be her brother. He's a family doctor who specializes in treating patients with chronic pain and mental health issues! Finally, I found someone who could help me. He changed a number of my drugs, and I finally got a break from the pain. He was calm and observant. He recommended a pain doctor, a rheumatologist, and a pain therapist. We agreed that he would be my primary prescriber. By the time I started seeing this amazing doctor, I had put on 100 pounds and was dependent on a cane to walk. I hurt 24/7.

Through all of my medical problems, life didn't just stop as I would've liked. By now, I had been declared disabled and put on Social Security, but that didn't even begin to cover my expenses. My parents paid my mortgage for an entire year. I couldn't take proper care of myself, much less my acre of property and my home. I often paid someone to mow the lawn or fix little things. I knew it was time to sell my house; it was just so hard for me to admit it. I was so proud that I was able to buy my own house after my divorce from Josh. At the time of my divorce, my credit was destroyed and I believed I would never own a home. Just five years later, I had near perfect credit, my dream car, and a fabulous home. I was so proud of both. Anyone who visited my home or saw my car said, "It fits you so perfectly," or "It's so you!" That's because "it" was chosen by me, for me, and decorated by me.

I felt depressed, sick, isolated and not even motivated to clean my home for showings, much less go through all of the motions of selling a house. One day, I was informed that a "family meeting" would take place at my home the following week. We'd *never* had a family meeting before. I was sure this was going to be an intervention about me staying home all the time, giving in to my pain and not taking good care of myself. They would say I was wallowing in my pain and fatigue. I prepared packets for all of my family members to read about fibromyalgia and depression, complete with symptoms, possible causes, what not to say to a fibromyalgia patient, and how to tell when I was truly depressed and a suicide risk, versus just feeling down or in pain.

I was so nervous about this meeting. I fully expected to be bombarded with things I should do differently. I was resigned to having to stand before my judge and jury. So imagine my shock when all four of my brothers, two sisters-in-law, and my parents showed up to simply say, "You need to sell your house." *Duh!* After all of my preparation and worry, our "family meeting" lasted all of five minutes.

Within two days, I retained a Realtor to do a short sale on my home. It was heartbreaking that I was going to lose the house I had worked so hard for, but it had to be done. After all, a house was just a possession—one I could no longer afford. My Realtor was a kind and knowledgeable woman. She explained to prospective buyers that I was sick and would be home for the showing, but I would stay on the couch and not interfere. After just a few showings, we received an offer. However, it all had to be approved by the banks that held my two mortgages. I chose my Realtor specifically because she knew all about short sales. It took a while, but she managed to navigate all of the hurdles and the sale was final.

During that time, my family was busy remodeling my brother Ryan's two-story lake home, so I could go there to live. I did *not* want to go and live there, but what other choice did I have? I responded that Ryan was a slob and that every inch of his home had stuff on it, except for the one place where he sat on the couch. My mother assured me that it would not be like that anymore. She said I needed to be closer to family so that they could help me. My brother John, and his wife Sandy, lived just four houses down the street with their two adult children. Sandy asked what colors I wanted for my bedroom and living room. I wanted my bedroom to be lavender so I could put the purple fibromyalgia butterfly on the wall. I went with just creams in the living room, with green accents. I hadn't seen the house since the previous summer, and that was only to go in quickly to get the keys to the pontoon boat. The clutter stressed me out so much I couldn't wait to get out. I was still *not* happy about having to leave my home and my solitude.

chapter 41

New Beginnings

When I took the first load of my things to Ryan's house, I was amazed! The whole house had been transformed and it looked great! I knew that my sister-in-law Sandy and my parents put a lot of time and money into the house—everything from new carpeting to new windows and doors. My niece, Shana, painted the fibromyalgia butterfly on my bedroom wall for me, and it was beautiful! I felt like a horrible aunt for not knowing she was so artistic. I was given my own space, including a bedroom, living room, bathroom, and small office area. Ryan and I planned to share the kitchen. We closed on the sale of my house in early August, and although we began the moving process little by little, everything was over to Ryan's long before the closing. A dear friend and fellow fibromyalgia patient, Lucy, and her husband provided much help during my move! I couldn't have done it without them. When Christine moved away earlier in the summer to be with her Prince Charming, I felt very alone. I didn't think I could pack up and move without her. I felt very lucky to meet new friends in Milwaukee who also had fibromyalgia. Lucy was one of them. Friends from my past also came back into my life. Loraine, my friend from seventh grade, and my former colleague, Gloria, both came to help me pack. Loraine told me she was bringing a friend of hers, who happened to live in my town. It was funny when I came home and saw that Loraine's friend was a woman I'd talked to often at the gym. We just didn't know one another's name. Gloria also brought her son, who was a big help.

Before I became truly ill, I attended a church that resonated with me. I only attended four or five times before I moved away. The church's pastor was kind enough to come and see me in the hospital when I was there. He also was kind enough to pick up some groceries for me when I couldn't get out of the house. I joined the church's "inclusion committee," which was focused on how the congregation would be best able to serve a diverse array of people, from the physically, emotionally, and developmentally handicapped to the gay and lesbian community. The woman who led the committee was a big support for me, as well. The church published one of my writings about the invisible illness in its newsletter. I was touched to get cards and emails from members of the church, thanking me for opening their eyes and for helping them to see that challenges are not always visible.

This is the writing the church published:

The People the World Forgot
by Bridgette

You may not notice us, though you see us all the time. You just don't know we're sick, because there are no outward signs. You might even yell at us, because we parked by a handicapped sign. What you don't know is that trips to the store take our precious, productive time. If we use the scooters, you think we're lazy or out to have a good time. "You're too young to need a scooter" is what some people say. I just smile and say, "I wish," as I continue on my way. What they don't know is this: Whether I use a scooter or not, by the time I get home, I can barely walk. Last week, I had to lie on my kitchen floor for twenty minutes before putting my groceries away. That would never occur to most people, because it's just a normal day.

There are many of us you don't see, because we're stuck at home. Friends stopped coming by a while after we got sick. It's not that they don't care at all; it's that they forget to call. "Out of sight, out of mind" is what I like to think. I have to, because thinking that my friends stopped caring would feel like my heart was tearing.

I try to keep my chin up and hope we find a cure. I do all the research I can, writing letters to high-level figures. Unfortunately, most invisible diseases are invisible to researchers, too. I guess there's no money in curing a disease that's not fatal. What most people don't realize is that many of us have already died. Our bodies still go through the motions, but our hearts have been many times broken. For those who still feel emotion, sometimes suicide seems like a valid notion. Families are losing loved ones and they'll never know why. One in five people with invisible illness can't live like this—and they prefer to die.

Many think we're lazy or prefer to be alone. Until you've walked in my shoes, please stop casting stones. Before this illness took my body, I was highly productive and still able to party. Now, most days I sit on my couch, waiting for the phone to ring or someone to visit. These things now happen less and less. Pretty soon, the world will forget me, I guess.

Although the writing seems depressing now, it was my reality at the time. It became clear that I could no longer function as a normal person. No matter how hard I tried, it was extremely difficult just to keep up with the house and feed myself. I had long since begun ordering my groceries from an online grocery store, and my cat food, litter, and softener salt were delivered by a local feed store. These deliveries were more than just helpful; they saved me from days of additional pain and fatigue. But, as with anything else, you pay for service. I couldn't afford luxuries like deliveries or lawn service, but I also couldn't do these things myself. While a couple members of my former fire department told me, "Call me if you need anything," I didn't have any support coming from that direction—and certainly not any from the sheriff's department! Kyle would have helped if he could have, but the horse farm he and his wife operated took all of their time. The farm, by itself, was pretty much a full-time job, and then Kyle still went to work. No solution allowed me to stay in my home.

The one good thing that Rainy did for me—and for Craig—when we worked for her was to send us to the Celebrate Your Life conference in

Phoenix where Dr. Wayne Dyer was the keynote speaker. I was introduced to Dr. Dyer when Craig loaned me the book, *You'll See It When You Believe It.* I was fascinated by that book, as well as by the principles of the Law of Attraction. Most people first heard about the Law of Attraction when Oprah promoted the book *The Secret.* However, many other books have been published on the subject. I read many of them after attending that Phoenix conference—and that's when I was able to get my new car, my new house, and my new job. Now that I was sick, I began to question my own mental health. I believed that I had attracted all of these bad things into my life through my own thoughts and energy. I worried about every thought I had for fear it would manifest itself into my reality. Momentum—good or bad—has a snowball effect. My momentum went from bad to worse during the past two-and-a-half years.

On my final moving day, I was awestruck at the people who showed up to help me move—not only my family and friends, but people from the church whom I'd never even met before. The move was both exhausting and traumatic for me. For the final transport of items from the old house, Lucy and I drove in separate vehicles, and I was exhausted, stressed, and in pain. Just as we passed the halfway point, I began to develop all of the classic symptoms of a heart attack. It began in my left arm, moved up into my shoulder, and into my neck and jaw. I had to make a decision: We were about to pass one of the top-rated heart centers in the world and the only hospital I was aware of between where we were and my new home. I called Lucy and advised her I was pulling off. She followed me to the hospital and sat with me in the E.R. while they ran an EKG and failed on the first eight attempts to start an intravenous line! Lucy called my parents and they immediately drove to the hospital. I was admitted for overnight monitoring and testing. The following day, I was sent for a stress test. Due to my physical limitations, the stress test was about the least stressful thing I've ever done. I was so tired that I practically slept through it. They injected a drug into my system to raise my heart rate, and monitored my response. The test was over before I knew it. I stayed one night, possibly two, and when I was released, I knew that I could no longer go "home." I was headed to Ryan's home, where I still had much work ahead of me.

I was once again blessed, as my family made the place habitable for me by arranging my furniture where it belonged, making my bed, and putting many of my things away. I settled right in and was able to get some rest. The transition to Ryan's house wasn't nearly as bad as I thought it would be. We each lived in our own space—and it was nice to have someone to share dinner with. I enjoyed cooking and Ryan made a killer steak on the grill! We both loved having someone to cook for and eat with.

Ryan never wanted a pet, so the way he took to my three cats was nothing short of a miracle! He loved them right from the start. He called me to look at what this cat or that cat was doing. He assumed the job of giving them their "treats" every night. (I only used to give treats to them about three times a week.) He even kept trying to get the youngest cat, Kibble, to eat a treat, because he felt guilty that the other two got treats and Kibble did not. Kibble got his name because he never ate anything other than dry food from the time he was three weeks old. (He was part of a litter that I raised after they were abandoned as babies. The rest of the litter loved their replacement milk and soft food, but Kibble didn't want any of that. Watching him eat was hysterical.) Ryan absolutely *loved* playing laser light with my middle cat, Cooper! He bought more laser lights in the first few months after I moved in than I ever had in my lifetime. And my oldest cat, Katie, took an immediate liking to Ryan. She always tried to get his attention. She held conversations with us as if she understood what we were saying, and then she responded to us in her own way. She ran downstairs every time she heard Ryan brushing his teeth, and then she "talked" to him while he continued.

chapter 42

With Each Ending Comes a New Beginning

Once I moved in, a huge burden was lifted from my shoulders! I no longer worried about how to pay the mortgage or how to care for the house. I was able to finally function as a person, and then I began to address many practical issues that I had ignored for a long time. For the entire previous year, I dreaded getting any mail, and I tended not to open it. I knew it would be a bill that I couldn't pay. By the time I moved in to Ryan's house, I had an entire suitcase of envelopes that I hadn't touched. Every time I tried, I was just paralyzed. I called on Lorraine to help me out yet again. She did far more than just help me out! She took paperwork home with her on at least three occasions. In the end, she returned all of the important documents to me fully organized and sorted, with some even placed into three-ring binders. What a relief: My "suitcase of shame" no longer existed.

I had a number of knee surgeries throughout my life, and it finally got to the point that gel injections were no longer helping me control the pain. My only option was a total knee replacement. My regular orthopedic doctor was not comfortable replacing a knee on someone so young. The doctor advised me to have my rheumatologist manage it. Her idea of "managing it" was to give me a boatload of Vicodin and tell me to wear a knee brace. I knew I couldn't live like that—not to mention, Vicodin is not effective for fibromyalgia patients. As my pain doctor explained it to me, Vicodin works on the pain receptors in the spinal cord, and fibromyalgia patients need medications that work on the pain receptors in the brain.

I remembered that many years earlier, when I assisted anesthesiologists in surgery, one surgeon did *a lot* of knee replacements. I made an appointment with him and contacted a friend from the fire department who sold artificial joints. My friend confirmed that the surgeon was the right choice. After he looked at my X-rays and MRIs, the surgeon said, "So, when do you want your new knee?" The surgery was scheduled for August 29. I was admitted to the hospital after all of my pre-op work was done. What I remembered about that hospital stay was my displeasure at how often physical and occupational therapists took me from my bed. The doctor required them to ensure that I could go up and down steps before I could be released. I came home after three days. Ryan was very helpful to me, and I had a refrigerator upstairs in case I couldn't make it down the steps.

My recovery went very well. I took part in physical therapy two to three times a week, up until the weekend of December 10. I overexerted myself that weekend and was knocked back a bit on my recovery. During my down time, I searched the Internet for positive role models and influences. I stumbled upon a class being offered online on "Mastering Change." If anyone needed to master change, I did. Tuition was $50, but the instructor offered sliding scale payments and scholarships. I applied for and was granted a scholarship immediately. I also stumbled upon an author who taught the Law of Attraction. He offered a private coaching group that met through a Facebook page with weekly conference calls. The cost to participate was $37 per month. I knew I couldn't justify that expense, because I was still borrowing money from my parents and brother just to get by. I wrote to the author, Hemal Radia, and explained my situation. He agreed to let me try the first month for just $5. I took him up on that offer and began visiting his Facebook page on a regular basis. I loved the energy there. Between the online dialogue and the calls, I began to feel hope again. Hemal was the person who walked me through the steps of how to publish a book, making this project more than just a dream. As I wrote my story, I listened as people told me how impossible it is for new authors to get published. The fact that you are reading these words right now tells you that anything is possible!

As the days went on, I found I preferred to spend more time in Hemal's group than in any of the fibromyalgia support groups. Even the group I started myself, as a place of education and support, was now depressing to me. I began to notice that most of the groups offered people an opportunity to complain about pain, fatigue, bad doctors, and how nobody understood their pain—rather than being a place of healing and support. I experienced a moment of clarity when I realized that I no longer wanted to live in a state of victimhood. I had power, I had hope, and I was going to learn to *live* with fibromyalgia rather than just exist. I chose to leave most of the fibromyalgia support groups, including the one I started myself. Many of the members of my group were upset when I announced I was leaving, but I reminded them that they could still reach out to me for support any time they chose.

My first month participating in Hemal's group was so successful that I used the Law of Attraction to manifest more than $280 from unexpected sources, as well as items people sent to me. As the "overachiever" in me reawakened, I began suggesting ways in which Hemal could market more items and be more profitable. I offered to do the legwork for him. Hemal and I hit it off so well that we agreed on an arrangement in which I would assist him with some administrative work in exchange for a private coaching package and membership in the group.

My life changed so dramatically during the past six months. I was barely recognizable. I no longer sat around staring blankly at a television screen all day. I wrote, talked with friends and others who needed support, did work for Hemal, and built my own brand. I realized that everything I experienced in my life led me to this place. I was destined to reach out, share my pain, and help others heal.

After my suicide attempt, I realized what kind of chemical changes the brain is capable of, and it was frightening! It showed me how dark that place was, taught me compassion, and allowed me to help others move from that dark place back into the light. I became *very* angry at the world after what had happened to me at the sheriff's department. I was especially frustrated when I realized that I was taken in by the advertising of my first lawyer, and I probably would have won my case if I had hired my second lawyer first. Sadly, by the time he got the case, my family was running out of money. We decided on a "stopping point"—and when we hit it, we let the matter go.

After my fibromyalgia diagnosis, I believed I was in a position to help find a cure and to support others. I wanted people to know that the suicide rate for fibromyalgia patients was far greater than the national average. Some statistics have shown that one in five fibromyalgia patients attempt or commit suicide. Women with fibromyalgia are ten times more likely to attempt suicide than those without fibromyalgia. These statistics were staggering! After doing some reading, I came up with what I believed could be a cure. I contacted a friend of a friend who was a neurologist and shared my idea with him. After some discussion, the doctor refined my original idea into Transcranial Magnetic Stimulation. Not only did it treat the symptoms, it allowed for brain mapping during the process. He believed it could work. Both of us contacted the company that made the necessary equipment, but we were dismissed as quickly as our messages were received.

I became very active on Facebook as an advocate for fibromyalgia patients and suicide prevention. Through my own Facebook pages, I also met a lot of other wonderful Facebook page administrators. There are many wonderful people out there who give of themselves day and night to offer hope and inspiration to others.

Facebook also gave me the opportunity to put to rest any doubts I had about men from my past. My first official boyfriend from my freshman year, Peter, connected with me on Facebook and told me he also was divorced. I always sensed he was flirting with me. Until I attended my first Fibromyalgia Awareness Event, no pictures of the "sick" me were available on Facebook. I told him I was sick, but I guess he still thought I looked like the woman in my old pictures. When I posted pictures from the fibromyalgia event that showed me at my heaviest, relying on a cane to walk, Peter told me how disappointed he was to see those pictures, and then he asked me if I knew whatever happened to two other girls he had crushes on in high school. I no longer felt any regret for hurting this insensitive narcissist! Brandon and I reconnected when we were in our late 30s. We went out once or twice and talked on the phone a lot. He turned out to be the same old Brandon. He made plans with me and then broke them. On the phone, all he talked about was how successful he was. I also suspected that he was an alcoholic. Narcissist number two: check. Tate and

I exchanged a few emails. He was more interested in talking about the sex we had than anything else. As I wrote this book, I pushed him to answer whether he really did love me that first summer—or not. The answer was that he really didn't know. After I hit him with more hard questions, he stopped answering my emails. I won't go so far as to call him narcissist number three. He was just a young man who was terrified of his feelings. I never talked again with my ex-husband, Josh, but I made contact with Josh's daughter Amelia. I wasn't surprised to learn that her dad had taken $1,200 she had saved for a family vacation and used it to abandon his house, let it go into foreclosure, and move across the country to Arizona with his third wife. (Shockingly, she's still with him!) I received a number of calls from creditors looking for him; I told them that Josh hasn't been my problem for more than a dozen years. I reconnected with Roger, the boyfriend I hurt after my senior year. I'm now comfortable that I made the right decision where he was concerned. We're good friends, but I don't think I could ever truly love him. I've often wondered about Christopher, the hot bartender I fell in love with at the bowling alley, and occasionally I tried to look him up. He became engaged just before I called off my wedding. According to records, they are still married.

Before I became sick, I also attended a reunion for the water-ski team's 50th Anniversary. I was looking my best and finally had the attention of the people I'd been trying to get to notice me so many years ago. It was not redeeming, as I realized they were not the kind of people who deserved MY attention. The flirting and jokes were rude and crude, and a lot of comments were made about my breasts. I was happy to leave them, feeling good about myself.

chapter 43

A Lesson in Forgiveness

*L*ooking back on my past, I am ashamed of much of my behavior, but I exposed it with the hope of helping others who have been "damaged" by guilt, insecurities, or traumatic events. Despite my shame, I have forgiven myself. I know that the God I believe in forgave my sins the moment I asked for forgiveness. If the Creator of all things can forgive me, why would I not forgive myself? I am certainly not a better judge of character than God!

As for my suicide attempt and my illness, I believe I was given those challenges to help prevent suicides and to remove the stigma of mental illness so that more people will seek help. Writing this book has helped me to heal. I've been able to merge my "damaged self" with my "higher self," and now I am on the path to becoming my Divine Self—the person I was meant to be all along. I've been able to let go of all past hurts and offer forgiveness to those who caused those hurts. Forgiveness is something that doesn't have to be announced. It has to be something you feel within yourself. I thought I'd long since released those hurts and held no more anger or animosity towards anyone, but I learned differently just this past week when I was offered a free session with an energy healer. She did not speak during our session; she just meditated. As I lay there in silence, I experienced many things. I felt that old anger and hurt—unaware that it still existed within me—and I felt it leave me, clearing up even more space within me to receive the gifts that continually come my way. I now feel nothing but compassion and unconditional love for people, including those who have hurt or greatly harmed me. My challenges have given me a platform and an opportunity to help thousands of people see themselves in me. I hope my words brought my story to life and that you have seen some aspect of yourself in me. I hope that you now know that it's okay to be "damaged." Everybody is. The key is to acknowledge that "damaged self" and forgive it. Merge it with your "higher self" and become the person you truly are.

Treat yourself with nothing but respect—and demand that others do the same. If a relationship does not serve you in a positive way, it's okay to let it fade away. When we learn to respect ourselves, no force in this universe can penetrate our resolve. Negativity ceases to exist. Our thoughts are the key that allows us to manifest everything in our lives. We use our thoughts to envision the future we want for ourselves, and it begins to happen just as it has for me. Resources and people have shown up in my life at just the right time. I have learned from each of them and have used them to create this body of work.

The key to finding happiness does not lie outside of you. It is within you. Dr. Wayne Dyer said, "When you change the way you look at things, the things you look at change." I've changed the way I view my life, and I now view everything from a place of gratitude. I've worked with my wonderful doctor to manage the effects of fibromyalgia, and I have continually reduced the number of medications I take. I now *live.*

One example of that occurred a few months ago when my aunt and uncle had an extra pair of tickets to the Wisconsin Badgers' game and offered them to my brother Ryan. My niece's boyfriend was a senior playing on the team. At first, Ryan hesitated in asking me to go, because he feared it would be too much walking for me. When he told me, I said that I'd like to try, but I didn't want to ruin his day if I wasn't able to manage it. Although I'd been walking without a cane for a while, I brought one along just to be safe. Ryan skipped meeting friends and taking part in pre-game festivities. We stopped along the way and bought a blanket and had breakfast. We managed to find parking and a shuttle bus that took us to the stadium. It was a pretty long walk to our gate from where we were dropped off, but I made it. We sat down fifteen minutes before kick-off. We sat next to our aunt and uncle, so it was nice to chat, too. I was astounded by how much more there is to see at a game compared to watching one on TV! The large marching band was incredible. I watched cheerleaders, a dance team, trainers, and the camera crews. It was so amazing to finally watch my niece's boyfriend play in his last college season! For about the first ten plays, I never even saw the ball. I just watched him do his thing, and I finally understood that he really was destined for the NFL. After the game, we were invited to the family area to wait for him. He and my niece were going to go out to dinner to celebrate their second anniversary. It took him forever to come out of the locker room, because the press was interviewing him. Once he came out, he was approached by agents who hoped to sign him. It was a lot for me to take in. Sadly, by then I was really hurting and was ready to go home! We waited for my brother John to drop the kids at their restaurant, because he was coming back to take us to our car. In the meantime, we walked four blocks to drop things off at my niece's boyfriend's apartment. It wasn't bad for a healthy person, but for me the short walk felt like miles. I don't regret it, though. It hurt like hell and was even worse the next day, but for just one day, I really *lived!*

I get out of the house more often now. I go to my parents' condo to swim. I shop. I go downstairs and cook dinner. I meet friends at restaurants. I also go outside just to be in the sunshine. I overlook the beautiful lake as I write each day. I have a cozy and homey place to live, and one that I love. I have a wonderful bond with my brother Ryan that I never had the opportunity to experience before. I feel like a human being again! I learned that a positive attitude and change of focus can make all the difference in the world. I still see a pain therapist and a pain doctor, in addition to my family physician, but I no longer need a cane or feel pain or fatigue on a regular basis. I've lost about half of the weight that I put on when I became sick, and I continue to lose more slowly, with the constant help of my dear dietician, Betty. Though I am not currently a client, she is still a friend who pushes me to at least weigh in weekly and email the results to her. I can't thank her enough for still caring so much about me—and my progress!

I plan to embark on a book-signing tour. I'd also like to take cooking classes and maybe even violin lessons in the near future. I enjoy the friends I've made on Facebook, in groups, and in life. I know that I won't have to live with Ryan forever. Eventually, I'll be able to afford to move into my own home again. In fact, I have my eye on a huge, beautiful lakefront home down the road. I can now honestly and wholeheartedly say: Life is good! (Christine, if you had any doubt at all, that last line is dedicated to you!)

PART 7

I am who I am

"As human beings, our greatness lies
not so much in being able to remake the world…
as in being able to remake ourselves." ~ **Mahatma Gandhi**

The original manuscript for this book was submitted for publishing on February 14, 2012. Since that time, my life has come a very long way! These are bonus chapters not included in the first edition.

chapter 44

Living It Up!

On February 27, I departed with my parents for an extended vacation. The original purpose of the trip was to take advantage of a cruise that was "gifted" to me by a friend. We elected to leave early and take a leisurely drive from Wisconsin down to Florida. Because of my excitement about the release of this book, and the demands of social media to market it, I kept my laptop within reach at all times. I also did a *lot* of communicating via my smart phone from the car. Despite staying "in contact" online, I still enjoyed every minute of the trip with my parents! I sat in the front seat while Dad drove. I took charge of the music. The three of us enjoyed being together, and the drive didn't put any stress on us at all. I also got a good laugh out of the fact that my parents, in their 70s and completely oblivious to modern technology, "schooled me" in finding the cheapest hotels along our route. While I was searching all of the last-minute travel and hotel websites, Mom and Dad insisted on stopping at a rest stop to grab the "discount magazine." I was blown away by the prices offered in these little gems! My technology couldn't touch them!

When we stopped at a hotel on the second night, I grabbed my backpack out from under my seat, only to discover that my *large* travel mug of water and lemonade had tipped and leaked all over the floor. My backpack was wet, and I was immediately worried about my computer. As soon as we got into our room, I fired up my laptop and gave a huge sigh of relief as I posted my blog. I also had a little fun with a "secret project." My dad has been driving cars and trucks for dealerships, companies and individuals since he retired about 15 years ago. He mentioned that it would be "neat" to have business cards. I have done *a lot* of online ordering and designing, so when Mom and Dad went to sleep, I designed and ordered Dad's business cards for him. He was *so* excited when I showed him what it looked like. Unfortunately, he didn't see it that next morning.

When I awoke and started my laptop, *nothing!* It would not power up at all. Frantic, I called my wonderful computer man back home, who created the framework of my website, and was an absolute angel for me during the writing process. His skills allowed me to meet my self-imposed deadline of getting the manuscript to the publisher on February 14. Without him, I would have lost at least a week due to laptop "down time." When I explained the situation, he told me I most likely would have to replace the computer. He also texted me the "specs" of what I should look for based on my needs. Since I couldn't afford to be without a computer for the remaining two to three weeks of our trip, Mom, Dad, and I made an unscheduled stop at Best Buy before heading over to my friend Noah's house in Siesta Key, Florida. Spending the money for a new laptop was not exactly the *best* way to start our vacation, but I confess: I did love my new "toy."

Best Buy was only minutes from the home of my longtime friend Noah, his wife Judy, and their three children. We arrived at their house in the late afternoon. It was *so* wonderful to see them after what had stretched into years. It's amazing how time can escape you as you get older! Noah and I talked to each other at least every couple of weeks for the past 23 years, so it was easy to "feel" like we'd seen each other far more recently than we had. That was immediately apparent when I saw their children! The last time I saw the family, their daughter was 3 years old. She is now a stunning, kind, and extremely intelligent girl of 9! I had never even seen the youngest boy, who is 4. The middle child was just a year and a half when I saw him last, and I told him how he had been my little "snuggle bug." He loved that, and immediately resumed that role.

The couple of days we spent with Noah and his family were a bit chaotic. They were doing some renovations to the house, so our stay ended up displacing everyone. Mom and Dad slept in the daughter's room, I slept in the boys' room, all three kids slept in Noah and Judy's room, and Noah and Judy slept in the lower level bedroom. (The lower level used to be a separate apartment. We would have stayed there, but due to the renovations, the bathroom on the lower level was not functional.)

I felt terrible for displacing everyone, but I was *so* happy to be with them! The kids were amazing! They all took to their guests like they had known us forever. They enjoyed having us read with them, help with homework, watch them rollerblade, and cuddle them in our laps. I fell in love with them instantly! Judy is a wonderful mother. She constantly ran the kids from gymnastics, to karate, to Chinese class and more activities. While we were there, Noah took us out on his boat through the intracoastal waterways, around through the Gulf of Mexico, and back home. We also docked at a waterfront restaurant for lunch and saw a dolphin come right up to the boat. That ride was one of the highlights of our vacation!

After two nights with our friends, we were ready to drive up to Tampa. We planned to board our cruise ship that next morning. I rented a scooter for the cruise, which we picked up in Sarasota. The amount of walking required on a cruise ship was still well beyond my physical limitations. Despite my intention of not being limited by fibromyalgia anymore, my "new" knee was on its own schedule. I was getting out, and was socializing again, but I still couldn't walk through an entire grocery store without having excruciating pain in my knee. I would need a scooter to get around on the ship and shore, and enjoy the trip. And enjoy I did!

The cruise was *fabulous!* First of all, my embarrassment about having to use a scooter immediately evaporated when I met a lovely family at the muster drill, a "fire drill" type of procedure that acquaints all cruise guests to emergency procedures should they be required. The woman I met had been in a scooter for some time, and she gave me all of the "tips and tricks." We ran into each other throughout the trip, and she and her family retold my story to others aboard. I swear, they gave my story and my book more public relations on that cruise than I did!

One afternoon, while sitting in a hot tub, I shared a bit of my story with another woman who also had a knee replacement. Not long after that woman left the hot tub, another woman came in and said, "I was told I should come and talk to you. We have a lot in common." As it turned out, this woman also had fibromyalgia. She asked some questions about anatomy, physiology, and treatments. Frankly, by now I've become a bit of an expert on fibromyalgia and treatment options for it. After we talked for a while, one of us mentioned writing a book. This woman had just published her first book—and mine was coming out soon! What were the odds of that? We exchanged cards later during the cruise, and when I returned home I received a lovely signed copy of her book. I also sent her one of mine.

The service, food, relaxation, and joy of this cruise were probably the best that I had ever experienced. While much of my praise was the result of outstanding service by the staff, even more of it was due to my newfound appreciation of being on a cruise at all. I had been homebound just six months before, and now I was given the opportunity to spend some quality time with my parents in their "golden years." Had this trip not been a gift from a dear friend, I never could have afforded to take it. I was in heaven every minute of every day.

When we disembarked from the ship, I was anxious to reconnect with the "virtual world." Onboard, I limited my computer time to just long enough to copy and paste my nightly blogs and do a quick check of my email. At fifty cents a minute, I certainly didn't want to take away from my vacation by spending time on the computer!

I opened my email on my phone just as we exited the parking lot. The *very* first thing I saw was a review of *Fallen Angel Rising*, by Readers Favorite. My book had not even been published yet, and I just received a *five-star* review! I read it aloud to Mom and Dad, and we all celebrated in the van. What an incredible feeling of validation! I believed in my story and my message from the beginning, but it was *amazing* to know that my story truly connected with that reviewer!

From Tampa, we drove up to Atlanta to spend a few days with my cousin Colleen. We decided that we would rather drive a very long day, and settle in at Colleen's in the late evening, than stop and spend another night in a hotel. The drive was long, but the welcome was worth it!

I hadn't seen Colleen since she came to stay with me after my suicide attempt. It felt like coming home! It also didn't hurt that this was the first time in two weeks that Mom and Dad and I could spread out a bit. Colleen's house is very large. Mom and Dad had their own little apartment on the lower level. Colleen and her boyfriend Scott have a master suite on the main level, and I had my choice of rooms on the second level. I picked a room that had a futon, love seats, and adjoining bathroom—and I could step out the door and overlook the great room and first floor. It was wonderful! It felt good to have a little "alone time" in my room and space to relax.

We arrived at Colleen's house on Thursday night, so we had the whole house to ourselves on Friday. It felt *fabulous* to sleep in, and then hide out in my own room for a while. Eventually, I made my way downstairs to join Mom for breakfast. Later, I made my way out to the hot tub, and Dad came out to join me. Mom lounged poolside and read a book. It was absolutely perfect! When Colleen and Scott came home from work, we ordered take-out. Colleen had a birthday party to go to that night, and she brought all of her girlfriends by the house to meet us. She was blessed with a wonderful group of neighbors and friends. The whole stay was wonderfully relaxing! We stayed with Colleen and Scott until Sunday morning and then made the drive back home. We were determined to drive straight through to Wisconsin rather than spend another night in a hotel. We made it home, and our trip was complete. I valued all of the time I got to spend with my parents! I knew they wouldn't be around forever, and I cherished every opportunity to be with them. The vacation was just one more chance to make great memories!

chapter 45

Back to Reality

Once we returned home, reality set back in. I had noticed some memory lapses that Dad had on the trip, but I had tried really hard not to dwell on it. A week or two after we returned home, Mom called to tell me that she was very concerned about him. She had been worried about Dad's memory for some time, but it seemed to worsen during and after the trip. Mom even mentioned that, on a couple of occasions, Dad had become belligerent. That's one word I'd never use to describe my father. But after recalling a couple of events from our trip, I agreed that he should see a neurologist. The hard part was getting him to agree.

Mom gave me the contact information for a neurologist who had been recommended to her. She didn't feel like shouldering this challenge, so she asked me to make the appointment. I called the particular clinic but it was not helpful; Dad couldn't be seen for months. If it was early stage Alzheimer's, I knew it was important to get him in as soon as possible. I called my fabulous doctor for a recommendation and, as usual, he came through. I made an appointment with the neurologist my doctor referred me to and informed my mom of the date and time. She asked that some of the kids come over and talk to Dad about it. I reached out to my brothers, hoping they would support Mom and me in talking to Dad, and we planned a time to do that.

Mom decided it would be best for her to talk to Dad alone in the morning. I was relieved to hear that, because I wasn't looking forward to "surprising him." Dad readily agreed to go for tests, and we all still dropped by that evening for dinner and a swim at their house.

On the day of the neurology appointment, I accompanied Mom and Dad to the office. I sat in on the cognitive exam. I caught on to the fact that Dad often cracked a joke to gain a little extra time to think. I sensed that the neurologist did, too. Surprisingly, I even had trouble answering some of his questions. When you don't work Monday through Friday, it's not always easy or important to remember what day it is.

In the end, the neurologist said Dad had some signs of minor cognitive impairment, but nothing that seemed alarming, given his age. Just to be thorough, he ordered an MRI. When we didn't hear back from the doctor for a while, we took the "no news is good news" approach. Dad seemed to improve significantly within a few weeks of settling back in at home. Eventually, Mom and Dad went back in to see the neurologist and all was deemed good.

chapter 46

Positive Reinforcements

At one point, I learned about an amazing speaker who is both a chiropractor and neuromicrobiologist. He combined the concepts of positive thinking, spirituality, and science to encourage self-healing. His name was Dr. Joe Dispenza, and I was very interested in what he had to say! I looked up his scheduled speaking engagements and discovered he was speaking at a conference in Chicago in June. It happened to be the same conference I had attended years ago with my colleague Craig: Celebrate Your Life! The event was possible for me to attend, as it was within driving distance. I contacted the conference organizers and was allowed to pay for the conference in monthly payments. I also let them know that I was looking for a roommate to split expenses if they knew of anyone. They did! They introduced me to a wonderful woman named Joy. Originally I made reservations at a hotel down the road, as the conference site was too expensive. Joy had reservations at the conference hotel already. Sharing a room with her put me much closer to the action. I reminded myself that my body still likes to be able to rest as needed due to the fibromyalgia. The change of hotels was a good thing.

After Joy and I chatted a few times, I was up one night thinking about ways to reduce expenses. I thought about one of the popular online booking sites that allowed you to bid on a certain level of hotel in a specific area. You aren't given the name of the hotel until they've accepted your bid. My research allowed me to be fairly certain that the conference hotel was the only four-star property in the area. On a hope and a prayer, I placed a bid to stay at a four-star property in that area. It was immediately confirmed! I was now booked at the conference hotel for almost half of what everyone else was paying! Needless to say, Joy also was overjoyed!

The conference was scheduled for early June. I still had my doubts about being able to walk through the entire conference, but renting a scooter was just too pricey. In May, I attended a graduation party for my niece. I began talking with an old friend of one of my brothers. She also was diagnosed with fibromyalgia, but she was fully functional. She spoke convincingly about her gluten-free diet. From the moment I was diagnosed, I received diet suggestions. If I had listened to all of them, the only thing left in my diet would be water. However, I heard enough people talk about the effects of gluten that I was willing to give it a try.

I did some reading, reached out to my dietician, Betty, for suggestions, and even found an app for my phone that allowed me to check ingredients in the grocery store. Within a few days, I was eating only gluten-free foods.

To say the difference was miraculous would be an understatement! I never believed that food could make *such* a difference. After only three days of gluten-free eating, the pain in my knee almost completely disappeared! I no longer needed to use the electric scooter at the grocery store. In fact, I walked just about as far as I wanted without extra pain! Before I changed my diet, I noticed when my knee didn't hurt, because pain was my "normal." After the dietary change, I began to notice when my knee did hurt, and then I reviewed what foods I had eaten. By the time the conference arrived in June, I no longer had any doubts about my ability to navigate the conference center without a scooter.

In the days leading up to the conference, I talked with a woman I met on Facebook named Lana. She wrote a book very similar to mine, and we became friends. I told her about the conference, and she decided to join me. I contacted Joy to make sure she was fine with adding a second roommate, and we were set for the weekend. I drove down on Thursday afternoon, because a "Pre-Conference Session" with one of my favorite authors, Alan Cohen, was scheduled on Friday morning. When Joy and Lana arrived, it was *so* amazing to meet them both in person. It felt as if we'd known each other forever! By the time we were all settled, I was ready to crash! I got a good night's sleep and was ready for morning.

I actually found my session with Alan Cohen challenging. Because I was a huge fan of his, and had read all of his books, I could practically answer the audience questions for him. Nonetheless, I still learned a lot from the session. One of the best nuggets of wisdom that I took away from Alan's talk was the "coin toss." Alan gave each of us a yellow coin. One side of the coin read, "Yes." The other read, "If it's not a 'hell yes' it's a 'hell no!'" Alan encouraged each of us to think about a decision we had been struggling with. Then he had us flip the coin to help us make up our minds. The lesson was not to do what the coin said, but to notice how you felt the moment the coin gave you an answer. The lesson was: Deep inside, we all know what we truly want. We just need to listen to that inner voice.

For the next three days I moved from one class to the next, gaining incredible energy and insight! I felt *so* uplifted. Every time I returned to the room, Lana was sitting on the bed "working." I was never exactly sure what she was working on, but wondered why she wasted a lot of time and money coming to Chicago for a conference that she wasn't attending. She mentioned a book she was working on that featured a number of Facebook page administrators. She also talked about the conference organizers and speakers as if she knew them all. She referred to them all by their first names, assuming I knew who she was talking about. I usually didn't. I know that she left the room numerous times, because she purchased some products from the vendors and had her photo taken with a number of the speakers.

chapter 47

The World Doesn't Come on a Silver Platter, but It Does Come with a Silver Lining

When the conference ended, I was happy to return to my home, my bed, and my kitties. I continued to work on my website and Facebook page. I also kept in touch with Lana. At the end of June, she told me I would be featured in her upcoming book and would receive a large advance in early August. That was incredible news, as I had been struggling to survive on Social Security since I was declared disabled in 2009! I was so excited about the news that I called my parents to share. My mom then allowed me to charge some concert tickets to her credit card so I could celebrate. I wanted tickets to this particular show for months, but they were out of my reach. Now, I was able to get great seats and go with a friend. The concert was the night of June 30.

I had a great time at the concert and returned home to write my blog before bed. As I opened my computer, my browser came up on my home page. I realized that it was now officially July 1, and an email from Readers Favorite was the announcement of finalists in the 2012 International Book Contest! I was fairly confident, but my stomach did a lot of twists and turns as I opened and then paged through the email. When I came to the "non-fiction autobiography" category, I screamed when I saw my name and book title. I screamed so loud that I was afraid I woke up my brother downstairs. I couldn't wait until morning so that I could tell my family and friends!

Almost immediately after I told Lana about the book news, she invited me to be a part of a world speaking tour that she was organizing. I was to start on the tour in October and continue for the next year and a half with some summer and holiday breaks. What an opportunity! Here I was, this newly published author with a message to share, and now I was being offered the chance to share that message with the world. In addition, I would make money doing so—not just money, *great* money!

All of that news came in a span of just under two weeks! I was walking on air! I did it! I built a brand that was going to allow me to work around my disability! And I inspired enough people that they deemed me worthy of sharing my message side by side with a host of inspirational and motivational speakers and writers! What could possibly be better than this? I was just handed the world on a silver platter! I shared this excitement and information with almost anyone who would listen!

A few days into this process, some nagging doubts began to creep in. Lana began to talk down to me, putting me down in a backhanded way. I didn't appreciate the way she spoke to me. She also insisted that I use my full name for the book and the tour. Lana said "Spirit" told her very clearly that I needed to do as she said. It came down to me using my last name in her book or being "cut" from the tour, so I agreed to use my last name. Later on, I tried to open a dialogue with her about it. I told Lana that it felt disrespectful for her to tell me that her messages from "Spirit" were more important than those I received from my *own* inner guidance. She was not open to any discussion. Other little signs led to my intuition telling me that this was not the right project for me. Sadly, I ignored my intuition, because I wanted the book and tour gig so badly.

One Friday night in early July, Lana was on the phone and I told her I had just ordered new luggage for the tour. She told me not to spend the money before I had it. I said, "Well, you said the advance is coming the first week in August, so I'll be able to pay off the credit card as soon as the bill comes." Then Lana used the opportunity to mention that she "decided not to sell the rights to the book, so there would be no advance." My panicked intake of breath made her extremely angry. She went on about my "lack mentality" and how I should not have spent the money before I had it. I responded that she told me to have faith and believe in her, so I did. We hung up the phone that night with a tension between us. I knew what was coming.

On Saturday, the situation disturbed me so much that I reached out to my mentor, Hemal Radia. I explained to him that I was allowing her to talk down to me simply because I did not want to miss the opportunity. He and I discussed the situation at length, and we agreed that, for now, I would keep my mouth shut and continue to allow the process to unfold, as it was for the greater good of getting my message out.

On Sunday, Lana posted a somewhat harsh message on the Facebook page for the tour speakers. She made a point of saying that she didn't need anyone with a "lack mentality" on the tour and that it had better stop now. She then encouraged the more "successful" speakers to share their insight on how to eliminate that mentality. I expected her to appreciate the fact that I accepted responsibility for my own "lack mentality," and I posted that I was "one of" the people Lana referred to. I explained to the other speakers that I had been struggling for a while, but was ready to transform that. Lana then responded with a bit of a "shot" back at me. She wrote that I was "like the person in church who thinks the preacher is speaking directly to her." She went on to say that I was not the only one. I replied by saying "that's why I said 'one of' instead of 'the one.'" A short time later, Lana left me a voicemail to call her. I couldn't answer at the time, because I was on another call. When I did call her back, Lana told me she was taking me off of the tour—and she became angry that I was upset with the news. After just a few sentences, she hung up on me.

The following Wednesday, Lana sent me a message saying she hoped I had "pulled back enough" to hear what she was saying. She said I might be ready to join the tour before next year if I kept working on myself. She also "ordered" me to not respond more than once to her message. My response included a sense of the hurt I felt, but it also was intended to be constructive. I explained that I heard her, but I didn't think she had heard me at all. I told her that the way she talked to me was not acceptable, and that when I had first brought that up, I wished she had tailored her communication style. This led her to cut me out of the book. By now, I no longer cared. What I wanted was to "cut" Lana from my life. And I did.

The day after I was cut from the book tour, I signed on to do a number of new projects including some feature stories, and a new edition of this book. I also extended my stay at the Miami International Book Fair, where this book will be on display for agents, publishers, and buyers from all over the world. That was just the beginning. I refocused my energy on the primary reason that I do all of this: healing others. I went back to my regular style of posting on my Facebook page and website and watched my audience grow.

Just over a week later, I received messages from a couple of the other speakers who told me that they also dropped out of the tour due to communication style, lack of direct answers, and contract language. Of the 33 original speakers, I believe fourteen were no longer participating. I don't know what's happening with the tour now or if it even *is* happening. I released it as a lesson and have not looked back. However, I kept in touch with some of the other speakers and we are planning to work together on an event in the near future. From every disappointment comes an opportunity.

chapter 48

Am I Healthy, Wealthy, and Successful?

*H*opefully, as you read this, I am speaking somewhere where I can help others heal. I would be lying if I told you that my world is now 100 percent perfect, no matter how many changes I've made. I still struggle financially, but I have faith that this too shall pass. I still struggle with my health, but I'm doing far better than I had been. Considering the fact that just a year ago I could not walk without a cane, it's pretty incredible to be able to tell you I just completed a landscaping makeover on the lakefront!

I still have challenges. Lately, the biggest one was related to my health. A while back, my primary care physician told me to find the best rheumatologist I could, and to make an appointment. In addition to fibromyalgia, he said I had numerous abnormalities in my blood work that indicated a strong and acute immune-system response. I researched the top 1 percent of rheumatologists in the country and found one in Chicago. My first appointment with him was on July 18. Prior to that appointment, I had blood drawn at a local lab per his request. When I saw him in July, he talked to me extensively, looked over my blood work, ordered even more, and told me to come back in four weeks. I had the labs drawn in his office immediately.

Less than a week later, I received the results of those labs. Being the medical geek that I am, I couldn't stop myself from looking up the cited abnormalities. The same three diseases kept popping up—and none of them were good. They were lupus (the best of the three), myosisis (when the immune system attacks healthy tissue, and the same disorder that killed my aunt), and cancer. None was a good choice. By the time I was scheduled to return to the rheumatologist, on August 15, I had been getting sicker by the day. One week before my appointment, I ended up in urgent care. Pending the results of all cultures, the urgent care doctor identified a urinary tract infection, strep throat, and a possible ear infection. He put me on an antibiotic to help with all three. When I saw the rheumatologist a week later, I was still feeling miserable!

Mom and Dad insisted on accompanying me to that visit. They knew my suspicions and wanted to be with me if the news was as bad as expected. (Of course, I felt guilty for even expecting bad news, because my philosophy now is to focus on the positive. I was afraid that my doubts would cause me to get the bad news I so feared.) Fortunately, the news was actually very good! I didn't have any of the autoimmune diseases that were suspected. While it was great news, it also meant that my doctors still didn't know the cause of my issues. As I write this very chapter, I have a CAT scan of my lungs, and ultrasound of my abdomen scheduled for tomorrow. I had put off writing the final chapters of this second edition with the hope of telling you that my medical concerns were all resolved. But life changes and evolves, and no person can properly write an ending to her own autobiography.

What I *can* say with absolute confidence is this: Whatever the future holds for me, there will be a purpose behind it. Either I will be healthy so I can continue sharing my message, or I will have another illness. If that is the case, it will be just one more opportunity to overcome adversity, and to connect with and inspire even more people.

Note: As this book is being released by Balboa Press in August of 2013, I have been declared "healthy." The abnormalities in my blood work and lingering problems with my knee were all corrected with a revision of that knee more than six months ago. I can now walk as far as I like, and am free from any worry about additional health problems.

chapter 49

What I've Learned, What I Believe,
and What's Next?

I am human. As such, I continue to grow and evolve. I've learned to see the lessons and the blessings in everything that's happened to me. I've learned that each person sees the world through his or her own filter, based on the life they have led. I can no more judge another for the path they walk than they can judge me for mine. I've also learned that it's not my place to judge someone for judging me. If they choose to judge me based on the things that I've been through, and the choices I've made, that does not diminish me—or my message—in any way. Judgment of others says nothing about the "judged" and everything about the "judge."

I've learned the art of forgiveness and unconditional love in ways that I didn't even know were possible! When I completed the first edition of this book, I honestly believed that I had forgiven others. Then, in another moment, on another day, I found myself thinking about them, and somehow, I experienced a new and elevated level of forgiveness and love. If you read the first edition of this book, you may have noticed that I changed the name of a "key player." In the first book, the sergeant was named "Sgt. Lardo." I guess it was obvious that I hadn't achieved a full level of forgiveness. In this book, I elected to change her name to "Sgt. Margo." That name is not only much softer, but it shows just how far I've come. I have released all malice towards her: I am grateful to her and feel compassion towards her. I realized that like every one of us, she too has her own filters and perceptions of the world. Something in her life must have caused her to both judge and fear my condition so strongly. Whatever that was, I hope she has found healing.

We all make what we believe are the best choices possible at the time we make them. Sure, hindsight is 20/20. We can all look back and see how other choices would have been better. But that's looking *back*. If we spend all of our time looking at the past, we miss the gifts of the present and the possibilities of the future. As we move forward, we grow, evolve, and turn our adversity into lessons, or "wisdom." The wisdom we have now is not the same wisdom we had when we were struggling through our adversity.

It's taken me a long time to discover exactly who I am, and I now like what I see when I look in the mirror. I no longer live by the labels or standards that others wish to place upon me. I live from a place of joy, passion, and a deep inner knowing. I know that I am on this earth to share my lessons and healing with those who need to hear what I have to say. I know that nothing happens by accident. If you are reading these words right now, you were meant to read them, just as I was meant to write them. There is value and healing in them for both of us.

I've learned to respect myself, *all* of me: the old, the new, the injured, the healed, the human, the Divine, the person I was, the person I am, and the person I will become. Part of that respect involves listening to my inner voice. To connect with that voice, I need simply to observe how something makes me feel. If I feel pressured, guilty, stressed, or uncomfortable, I am not acting on my inner voice. If I feel joy, passion, happiness, peace, or a sense of wholeness, I am honoring my inner voice—and I am *truly* respecting myself.

I finally understand to the fullest extent possible that: "We all deserve to be treated with nothing but respect. In order to command respect from others, we must first and foremost respect ourselves."

With my Unconditional Love and Gratitude,
Bridgette

appendix

Final thoughts on Depression & Suicide

(I hope this helps you or someone you love. Feel free to copy and share this section with others!)

Most people are familiar with cars. While you may not know how to fix them, you know that some things are required so they run properly. First of all, they need gas. Without it, your car is going nowhere.

Cars need oil. If you run low on oil, the car won't run properly, and eventually the engine will blow. Cars also need anti-freeze or coolant. Without it, the car will overheat, start smoking, and eventually the engine will be damaged. In addition to all of the above, cars need brakes and power steering fluid, and they need an electrical system, including a battery, wiring, and spark plugs.

Without any of these essential elements, our cars won't run, or else they will seriously malfunction.

The human brain runs much like a car, except that your body automatically produces and fills it up with all of the essential chemicals, hormones, sugar, circuitry, and connectors.

So what happens when the body or the brain is not producing enough of these essential elements?

You probably have seen movies featuring people who see or hear things that aren't there. It's been proven that this really happens. But sometimes, there are more subtle signs and signals that the brain doesn't have the right stuff to run properly. Depression is one such symptom of that.

We've all felt sad when bad things happen, such as when we lose a friend or loved one. Sometimes we're sad for no apparent reason at all. Sadness is normal. Crying, talking, and expressing that sadness are all ways of dealing with it. But when does sadness become something more?

The signs of depression can be subtle at first. Perhaps you're just tired, and you don't feel like doing things you used to like. Maybe you feel lonely or alone, even when you're around other people. When you start to notice that you're feeling sad more often than you're feeling happy, pay attention and make a note! This might be a sign that your "fluids" are starting to run low or your electrical system has a problem. When these feelings last longer than a week, pay very close attention! This might be a good time to talk to a parent, counselor, or doctor.

Often, we judge ourselves when we are depressed. We're angry that we can't just "think happy thoughts" and make it go away. We may feel like we've failed ourselves and don't want anyone else to know. When these thoughts start to come, it's time to really pay attention. It's possible that our power steering fluid is very low and we no longer have control of the car. The problem is, we don't know it yet.

In the same way that a car malfunctions when it's missing something, the brain malfunctions, as well. Unfortunately, it's the only brain we have and there's no built-in mechanic to tell us it's not functioning as it should. We continue driving through life, but we've lost our steering, our brakes, and even our GPS.

It's important to know that thoughts of suicide are *not* normal. While a brief thought may cross everyone's mind at some point, when we have repeated thoughts of suicide, plan it out in our minds or begin to think it is a good idea, that is a *major* red flag that we're running low on something very important! It's important to pay attention and think to yourself, "My car has never run like this before. The fact that it's doing so now means the 'check engine' light is on and I'm headed directly for the ditch. I need help!" The first thing you need to do is stop the car! The moment you realize you're giving the option of suicide any serious thought or attention, stop whatever you're doing and go directly to talk with someone: a friend, family member, counselor, or teacher. The next thing to do is to call in that master mechanic—a doctor. Only a doctor can run the tests to identify what fluids are low. It's not going to be gas or oil; it will be a hormone like serotonin or nor-epinephrine, or a problem with the thyroid gland, or any number of other possibilities. The only way to know for sure is to have the car tested. You wouldn't drive a car if you knew it was unsafe and could kill you. Give your body the same respect.

When we learn that someone attempted or committed suicide, we wonder "what could be so bad that they felt taking their life was a better choice." Unfortunately, when your brain is not getting what it needs to run effectively, *everything* is that bad. You have difficulty solving problems. Even the smallest tasks seem like enormous obstacles. Sadly, you don't realize this is a malfunction that may be fixed with a thorough inspection or tune-up. You believe the car is useless and should be junked.

For those of you who know someone suffering from depression, or someone who's attempted or committed suicide, it's important to understand that the "person" doing those things isn't the same person you know. That person is buried beneath the wreckage of the malfunctioning brain. You think they're being selfish. Their mind believes they're doing what's best for everyone. You can't understand how they could do this to you, their family or friends. They probably aren't even aware that you'll be upset, because they can't think past that horrible dark place of pain. These people do not need our judgment. Trust me, they're doing more than enough judging of themselves for all of us. What they need is understanding, caring, empathy, and help.

I have been to this place. It's a place that very few people who are still alive have seen. It's a place of hopelessness, darkness, sadness, and pain. All you can think of is how to make it end. You believe you've failed because you can't pull yourself out of the misery. Sadly, you don't know that these thoughts are all a result of malfunction. You believe them to be fact—and they become the primary focus of your life. But, if you know it is a malfunction, then you also know it is okay to get help. You know that having these thoughts doesn't make you a bad person. You know that you don't have to hide these feelings or be ashamed of them. If you can bring these thoughts out into the open, the light will begin to shine on them and the darkness won't seem so vast.

Before the sunrise, there is just a sliver of light. Just that sliver is enough to bring the world from darkness to light, from night to day. If you know someone who's in a dark place, offer your hand to pull them into the light. If you're the one in the darkness, know that morning always comes—and all it takes to bring some light into your life is to open that cell phone and call for help. I've been pulled from the darkness and have been given the rare insight into what it's like to be there. I believe I was given this gift to educate others and to offer my light whenever possible. Please do the same and share your light.

Bridgette

ABOUT THE AUTHOR

Dear Readers,

This section is supposed to tell you all about me. However, since this is autobiography, you'll learn more than you ever wanted to know about me by reading it.

I will tell you *why* I decided to expose my entire life and all of the "skeletons in my closet" to the world: I am here simply to heal others. For many years, I believed I was serving that purpose as an Emergency Medical Technician. When that was taken from me, I wondered why I was still here. How could God take my purpose while leaving me on this earth?

Then, as I came through my darkest days, I began to write. By writing from a place of authenticity, sharing both the darkness and the light I've experienced, and discussing how I've managed to overcome it all, I realized that I could offer hope and healing to many. I could help others avoid the mistakes I've made, and shed the false beliefs I once held.

I learned that my gift of healing was never taken from me at all. Through adversity, it was magnified. I no longer heal with my hands. I heal with my words. I no longer heal one person at a time. I heal many. This is a gift I would not trade for anything. As wonderful as the awards and accolades for this book have been, they cannot compare to the messages I've received from people who had given up hope only to find it again; from people who thought they were alone in their shame, but now understand that shame was never theirs to carry. In offering my own story as my gift to you, I have been given a greater gift than anything I could ever have dreamed of; the gift of knowing I made a difference. I've never cherished anything more.

With Love and Light,
Bridgette

Printed in the United States
By Bookmasters